PROTOTYP

(2024)

CONTENTS

Irina Sadóvina (4–12)
- from *Pampalche*

**Zsuzsanna Gahse, trans.
Katy Derbyshire (13–15)**
- from *Bergisch teils farblos*

Lucy Mercer (16–19)
- Green, Relentlessly
- Eremacausis

Imogen Cassels (20–21)
- Rive
- New Song

Hasib Hourani (22–25)
- from *rock flight*

Jen Carter (26–28)
- from *Trinkets*

Agnieszka Szczotka (29–34)
- Occhio per Occhio

Miruna Fulgeanu (35–37)
- New Tattoo (Motivational Quote)

Rozie Kelly (38–45)
- from *Salt Tooth*

Louis Bailey (46–53)
- from *The Night Run*

Dominic J. Jaeckle (54–59)
- A Flower for Laura Lee Burroughs (Magnolia or Redbud)

Aria Hughes-Liebling (60–65)
- from *The Lesser Mysteries*

Eiffel Gao (66–73)
- A Thousand Miles of My Country by Wang Xi Meng
- In the End
- 光 / 塵   Light / Dust
- Ode to Light

Jacqueline Rose (74–78)
- Ink Play #1–4

Helena Fornells Nadal (79–82)
- SAINTS

Alex Mepham (83–85)
- Live in Truth
- Apostate Encounters the Rat Virgin
- Apostate Addressed by the Voices

Stephen Watts (86–87)
- Men Drinking Together
- Half An Hour In The Thomas Neale

Leonie Rushforth (88–90)
- Moon Setting
- Floods
- A Drowning

Oisín Roberts (91–94)
- Double Life

Mica Georgis (95–102)
- from *Oh...Mallards!!*

Galia Admoni (103–106)
- On Sunday 30th April at the Tate Modern...
- Further evidence that you are a true agent of chaos
- Confetti as instruction

Eloise Bennett (107–110)
- ☄✳ sky-watching with RA Walden's *access points*

James Rodker (111–115)
- RELIQUARY TRANSLATIONS, GLIMPSES (18 - 20 - 29 - 32)

Duncan Montgomery (116–121)
- Ever is the eye
- Sir Gawain & the Green Knight
- Three blue plaques for Samuel Palmer

Jordan Hayward (122–130)
- The One with Ross's Teeth
- The One with the Routine
- The One with the Apothecary Table
- The One Where Ross Meets Elizabeth's Dad

Matthew Halliday (131–135)
- from *Revelations*

Angélica Pina Lèbre (136)
- What is she to me?

Jack Young (137–140)
- TUMBA TYMBUS TOMBA TOMBA T'UMB TOMM TOMBE

Rochelle Roberts (141–146)
- from *Divination*

Maya Uppal (147–153)
- from *Museum = Time Machine*

c.f. prior (154–156)
- Delaying, lingering, residing: an essay in four rooms

Kat Chimonides (157–161)
- from *On Feeling Seen*

Kate Zambreno (162–166)
- Appendix K: Museum of The History of Human Suffering

Contributor Biographies (168–174)

Irina Sadóvina

—

from *Pampalche*

A Living

Pampalche grows up motherless and hardworking. She and her elderly father survive on the edge of the forest. Perhaps it's the lack of neighbours that is their undoing. All accounts of the past emphasise the importance of living together: you need a village to celebrate the coming of spring, to build a barn, to pay the cowherd's salary. A hundred villages to wage a war. A city on a hill to drown enemy boats. The entire Mari people to offer effective prayers in a sacred grove. But Pampalche and her father live alone.

    The father is an able man, a natural in the forest. Every day he gets up early to check the nets for fish and the traps for martens, while Pampalche goes out looking for burdock roots, raspberries, nettle leaves. Her beauty is that of a healthy animal: sturdy shoulders, broad bones, and astonishing teeth that catch the light when she speaks or sings.

    It's high summer. Pampalche's father steps out of the house after a downpour. The forest is drenched in sunshine. The birds sing, the snakes rustle. He listens respectfully, but he can't linger: if he wants to bring something edible back, he must go further along the riverbank, far beyond the soothing sounds of his kin. His step is light. All day long, he criss-crosses the forest. The traps have worked. It's a lucky day.

    Pampalche, meanwhile, is out in a clearing that is glorious green and red with wild strawberries. She stands still and listens for the cuckoo.

    tell me
    she asks the cuckoo
    how will my life go
    and in the following silence her question sounds like the ringing of little bells. Pampalche looks up and sees a hawk. She can make out its grey beak and its wide wings lined with white.

    When dusk falls, Pampalche's father makes his way back along the river. He's thirsty, he walks down to the water and leans forward for a drink. This is when things go wrong. The moment his lips touch the surface, a hand rises from the dark depths and grasps him by the beard.

Immobilised, breathless, the man offers a prayer:
the Great Good One of Water, do not let me perish
but the grip is tight. An answer rises from the surface, evaporates into the air around him and burrows into his mind:
what about all the fishing, all the fish? pay up
As his vision darkens, Pampalche's father croaks:
yes, yes, let me live

pay back with one daughter
hums the air.
Pampalche's father is quick to agree:
my maiden daughter, of the Silver Teeth
In an instant he is released from the terrible pull and is alone on the riverbank. On the way home, he weeps. Everyone must marry sometime, but maybe not like this. Not as repayment. Not to a river. All of this is horrible, strange, and inimical to life.

)

River

The Yul separates Mari Land into the fertile and cosmopolitan right bank and the wild, marshy left bank. Much of the historical material we have about the Mari amounts to exasperated letters written by priests dispatched to the Yul wilds in the seventeenth century. This is what they tell us about the river.

On the right bank, in Hill Mari country, things and people are on the move. Church bells ring at five in the morning. Ships come in throughout the day. Locals go out to the market and work at the docks alongside the Tatars, the Russians and the Chuvash. They wear crosses on wide chains like strips of chainmail. A few crosses too many – these people love to drape themselves in silver – but crosses nonetheless. Things are going well. The fields are plentiful, and the people know God.

But take a boat across the river, the priests write, and everything changes. The further you go the worse it gets: the thicker the forest, the wilder, dirtier, more illiterate the people, the bloodier the rituals. Unthinkable. Hundreds of geese, hundreds of goats, hundreds of horses, blood flowing along the birches, despite all prohibitions, and it is impossible to change their minds.

As Western priests and soldiers trickle through, plant fortresses on banks of small and big rivers, collect money, consecrate land for monasteries, cut off paths to beehives, Pampalche's ancestors go further into the forest, and become Meadow folk. To keep them in check, the Tzar's fortress is built, and grows into a city where four centuries later she will be born.

Pampalche's city, like all cities, has a centripetal force.

Connecting the Mari taiga with the distant capital of the big world, the city houses merchants, soldiers, officials, and other literate Russians, some of whom become friendly and help Mari peasants compose letters of grievance addressed to the Tzar:

our land was taken away by the monks
the soldiers abuse us
these used to be our beehives

In a word, not everyone likes the new fortresses springing up all along the river. Some are altogether repelled. Many Maris who speak the Meadow language set off eastwards, aiming for the Ural Mountains, as their adventurous predecessors did in centuries past. There, they mingle with Turkic-speaking peoples, adopt brightly-coloured threads, and perfect a faster-paced dance style. Moving eastwards makes sense: these Maris are following the familiar golden glow of the recently collapsed khanate. In its heyday, it drew most Yul dwellers, whatever their religion or language, into a thoroughly administered, tax-supported, functional whole.

Though let's be honest, Pampalche's city, like all cities, is as much about connection as it is about division. Starting out as it did, as an outpost of strangers, it has a modernising streak, which drives it to change with the environment. Since it is a city, it must turn like a weathervane following the currents of power.

But – curse and blessing – this city is too far from the centre's furnace where states disintegrate and come together again, sending out spectacular flares. This city sinks into the marsh. The forest infiltrates its walls.

)

Pampalche's Records

Pampalche counts her silver:

shiy pamash

shiy yomak

shiy kalyk

shiy keche

A silver spring, a silver tale, a silver people, a silver sun. Clanging silver, grey silver, silver coins weighing down a woman's chest. What can silver coins pay for? A wedding. A gun. Pampalche covers her teeth with tar and loses her beauty.

Father

On the way to work, Pampalche calls her father on the phone. Over the course of the past week, she has convinced herself that he is dying and will be dead any minute, all because of her frozen heart and her withholding of daughterly affection. But it is her father who maintains the distance. He is slippery like one of his leeches that hang off the skin during bloodletting. Pampalche's father is too naturally animated to be cold; what he does instead is deflect. Joke follows joke, non sequiturs pile up. Before long, she begins to feel not guilty but angry.

She tries to bring up her fears. What if she never sees him again? Things are too complicated. In fact, things have been blown up. She is stuck abroad, and the curtain between them seems to have fallen decisively this time. Pampalche's father doesn't want to acknowledge that her compulsion to leave home has always resulted in being separated when disaster strikes. He doesn't want to discuss the possibility of her return. He doesn't like to talk about disappointment. Maybe he no longer feels it.

Growing up asthmatic in an underground hut, he's gone as far in the Mari world as a person can. He's been an activist, a freelance creative, a local TV host, a government official. Pampalche has watched him be celebrated, forgotten, blacklisted, derided as a sell-out, persecuted as a radical. On and on turns the wheel of fortune, her father strapped to its side. Love and rage blind her when she looks at him directly, but when she is talking to others about him, she can articulate what she feels about her father and why. In his peregrinations, he's learned things that she is learning still. Full to the brim with a loser's wisdom, her father seems detached from big worldly concerns and invests in small things instead: saving enough to provide for relatives when he dies, installing street signs in grammatically correct Mari, saying words of mourning and consolation to Mari families who lost children to the Moloch of empire.

Pampalche's father has no patience for her growing pains. But she is sad that they don't talk. She wishes he could name the harsh truths that have made him harden. She still doesn't know how to hold them. She begins every day with writing down the list of things she knows: who is bombed, who does the bombing, who's been tricked or pushed into murder, who is starving, who is hiding in the forest, who flees and is stuck for eternity on a sleepless train ride. Truths pile up: who was beheaded. Who was castrated. Who was fucked and left for dead. She must learn to love without hope.

(

A Wedding in the Forest

Pampalche is neither the first nor the last to set off into the forest. The thicket is dense and unwalkable, but she runs, she's in a hurry, and, though struck by branches and slashed by thorns, she feels joy. As Pampalche gets further away from her home, her own wedding train moves in the opposite direction, towards her. Inevitably, their paths cross.

First, she meets a group of young men playing bagpipes. The bagpipes are a hundred years old, and they sound like the temples of Assyria, like the cries of an ancient animal. They have one sure aim, to pluck her out of her father's arms. Pampalche will evade them.

Then she meets a group of old men playing drums. They strike the leather softly, but the rhythm falls fast and hard. They have one true purpose, to drag Pampalche out of her father's house. Pampalche will thwart them.

Finally, she meets a group of women who dance. Their arms smooth out the disturbed air around them. Their steps are quick like the steps of a charging boar. They have one clear goal: to pull Pampalche's hair into a braided topknot and cover her crown with an unearthly shymaksh: long like the river, embroidered with seaweed. Pampalche will trick them.

Pampalche passes through. She is just another face in the crowd. Nobody can know her. It's not that she is not pretty without her silver teeth, but she is no longer Shiy Pampalche. She looks each of the revellers straight in the eye and asks:

where are you going?
whose wedding is this?
is this a wedding?

Turns out she enjoys risky behaviour. Maybe she wouldn't mind a scandal. But the guests are too condescending to notice that she is laughing under all that tar, and she slips through the wedding unrecognised.

Bees

Honey-hunting is a type of wild beekeeping, permacultural in spirit. Humans have long lived with the bees as the bees made their homes in the trees. All your ancestors did that, and so did Pampalche's. But by the time her mother was born, it was no longer possible to travel such long distances just to get to the family bees. So the bees were moved into wooden boxes, closer to home.

that's where your grandfather kept the bees
said Pampalche's mother
when they start asking you who you are, you can tell them that, that your grandfather kept bees.

Grandfather's bees are now dead. As a little girl, Pampalche's mother was stung by one of them and went into anaphylactic shock. She was revived with a generous helping of vodka and taken to the hospital. Pampalche's grandmother decided then and there to get rid of the bees for good, so when autumn came, the beehives were left uncovered.

all of them died
said Pampalche's mother with sadness.

Well, so much for age-old traditions. Pity the Shtramari bees whose world ended all those years ago so Pampalche's girl-mother could live. But conditions change. Bees freeze and starve. In the forest between the road to Ozan and the road to Kakshan, trees lie in heaps of blackened coal.

But we'll be alright, thinks Pampalche. Our ancestral wisdom isn't about reviving what must die. Instead, it's this: when nothing else can hold us, we can reach, above all other powers, for the power of retreat. This is why we always lived far from the river and the road. We don't need their futures. We are thinking about something else: miles away, days and nights of walking, ever deeper into the forest, where we used to keep our bees.

Zsuzsanna Gahse (trans. Katy Derbyshire)
—
from *Bergisch teils farblos*

1
The mountains are kneeling, even the three-thousanders and two-thousanders crouching and kneeling, and they pounce in the process. From inside a moving car, barely anyone will register the graunching and grinding in the rocky slopes, I assume, but a falling chunk of stone will suddenly hit the car roof, beneath which I'll be squashed flat after a short, sharp shock.

4
Where is the wit in the mountains? Forget it.

53
Before Sam's departure for London, the three of us were on the Grossglockner. Sam, the dog and I were on one of the less-frequented paths, ahead of us a man in an anorak, kitted out with good mountain boots, very well kitted, his rather light-looking rucksack dangling from his back. We had him ahead of us for a while, then he turned left off the path, slipped — we saw that much — and then after his misstep we saw him no more.

93
Someone gets resettled, and now he's there, there he is, says Manu. From Lake Lucerne to Greenland, from Angola to Kyiv, where he learns the meaning of fear, from New York to Bergisch Gladbach. Or someone moves from Cairo to the Alps, then to London and back to the Alps. Relocations like that would work well in a flip book.

94
And amid the mountains stand rock-acquirers, rock-obtainers, rock-getters.

228

Practice, training, drill, to get to like the Matterhorn. Exposure to the mountain is a purely therapeutic exercise. Close your eyes and listen for a possible echo. The idea is not to turn away heartlessly from the Matterhorn. If those in training still dislike the mountain after the exercise, they will be out of pocket, time wasted; but first of all they should expose themselves to it. They should close their eyes in the face of the big white mountain horn that they do not wish to climb, and develop a feeling for the innards of the mountain. On the inside of this rough hulk there are minerals. They should take no notice of the people arrived from abroad and standing alongside them, looking up at the horn and exclaiming Oh wonderful. These travellers have adjusted to the circumstances before they travelled, force-fed Wonderful and unable to see for real. They think the white horn is called Wonderful. The real practitioners, however, want to overcome their heartlessness; their practice means turning to face the mountain, turning to face it is all a matter of practice, and then they will manage the first step. They wonder how long this hulk might have been there. The rest remains open.

378

Autumn in the Alps, as early as August. Several shops are vacant in all the villages (self-echo, I have mentioned it before). Sam calls Manu's photo space, a former newsagent, a clink, a jail in other words, but transforming a paper shop into a workplace for photos is not a bad solution. From her clink, she can photograph the development of the other shops. There will be autumn shots, an Alpine autumn in mid-August, pensive and foggy, appealing; it will take some getting used to.

379

In this favourable weather, an American arrives in Zürich by private jet, flanked by two bodyguards. A civilised entrance. This landing is followed by a drive to Bündnerland.

380

In a crossword puzzle, I came across the word vassals; these would be the bodyguards, essentially. The American, a New Yorker, lands with his protectors to consult an architect in Bündnerland. They consult about extending an existing chalet and plans for a new, larger building. The bodyguards carry guns, the New Yorker (with the architect) will take possession of an area in the Alps, and the architect will complete a work of art with the project. This description is complicated because it is about a New Yorker, about his property in the Alps, and at the same time about the architect's artwork, about vassals who might possibly shoot, and that does not yet even cover all aspects; to what extent are the resulting buildings an artwork, and is a property in the Alps an asset on paper: a stock or a share? What happens to the owner of the Alps, and is the New Yorker with his guards and his architect simply a rock-getter tied up in an internet game?

)

Bergisch is a kind of multiple journal, so any selection
– from a total of 515 fragments – can only show certain aspects of the book.

Lucy Mercer

—

Green, Relentlessly

A bee parts each
clover petal quickly
as if searching for keys
in a stack of white towels
in the green resort
where she works
there isn't much time
not for the grass
Grass of Governance
and Securities
raising subjects into
over-illuminated air
no rest without visibility
the globes of the clovers
(soaked pink at the base
with the dead
she moves over them
like a call vibrating
on silent next to me
over the half-eaten leaves
tie-dyed with a single
knot the light–
green line of absence
half-ways from the green
centre. I have seen
how a net hangs over
the shadow world
drops caught on it
like jewelled clovers
that expert cutters
separated out
in a heist
many times yes

but they're replicas
only replicas
of ash –
won't you please lie
still...

)

Eremacausis

Two baskets
of hallucinogenic
geraniums move
up & down as
if on a wave
grey dust
in the corners
of the windows
I don't know
how it's done
only that it arises
a blue cloth moves
behind the window
extracting dust
as if from ichor
the fluid that wakes
(the transparent screen
as when I sensed
the sound of a bright
& most brittle
percussive instrument
& said nothing
or agreed
& now you're doing
the same for me?
do these geraniums
look like cranes
or storks
waves of air
what prosperity comes
in the humus, humorous
mutter? we were
unconscious upon
the surface
like origami at rest

the television telling
a courtroom drama
you liked
vanishing your terror
of the unlawful
world of dust
let me
tell you a joke
I alone saw
two women walk
into the dust
the first says is
this a joke
and the second says

)

Imogen Cassels

—

Rive

Cannot hear the donnée for the dry season
now, slow wading through
language's green water, having
finished. I looked down into
the grey star of my heart. I will fill
his hand with my back. And other
lines. More dead move, fraying into Spring.

Character arched away like a bridge
under itself. A tiny figure coursing
unbelievably fast towards
the arms of weeds; excised taken
home. And the false hazel, these bright
carvings, the art of losing tracing
(its cognac band about Life.

New song

When I am in love with freezing dew—
when I am in your neck,
or hanging in the crook of your arm
like the dark star of a port—
my observers tell me
I am a brilliant, modern sleeper.
Particularly there by the back windows
in the scarcing light
as a shallow fig leaf padded out with ice.
The rain was still drifting like it still
didn't think of itself, between
the tunnel gallery
and no present home.

Each want is past having,
which is why I wanted it.
The weather is a curtain
that never rises. The child released
like a spring, God's profile;
a stern inclusion. What,
after all, do you move across
your own polar silk road?
Brown diamonds the size
of one of my green orbs.
Smock honey. Raffia. Blitzed swans,
hungry as May. More night.

I clipped down and found
another level of bone,
only more worn, and stencilled:
when I am in your wrist.
I don't think beauty
could explain it for you,
wherever you are, whoever.
If I am a prisoner
in my own mind anyway,
it is a good mind. And said,
I had a life; which was
a wound; which would not shut.

Hasib Hourani
—

from *rock flight*

HOW TO MAKE A ROCK:
please find a piece of paper

ONE
scrunch it up

TWO
throw it

(

HOW TO HOLD YOUR BREATH:

ONE
take your right hand
use your index finger and your thumb
to pinch your nostrils shut

TWO
take your left hand
place the palm over your mouth
use lots of force to make sure
no air can come in or out

THREE
make your lungs stop moving

NOTE
if you are my mother don't worry about steps ONE through THREE you
know how to hold your breath without doing anything at all   )

HOW TO MAKE A BOX:

please find a piece of paper

ONE

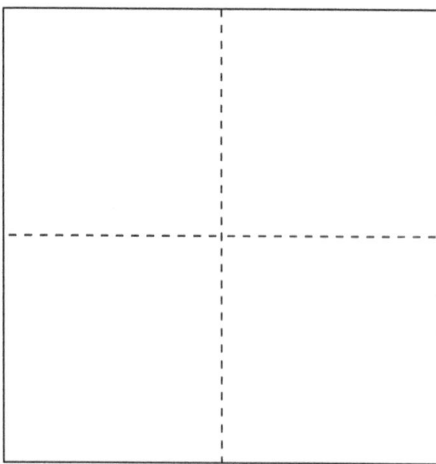

fold the paper in half one way
then fold it in half the other way

TWO

use the grooves from step one and
fold the corners into the centre

THREE

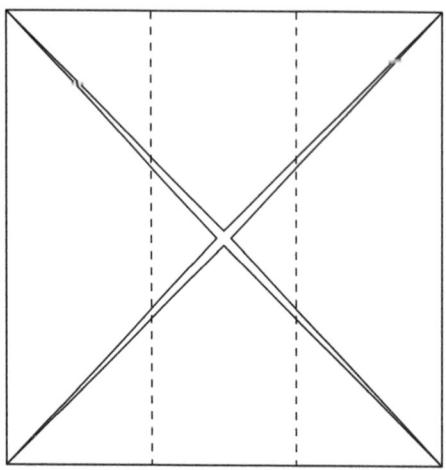

fold the new smaller square into
thirds one way

FOUR

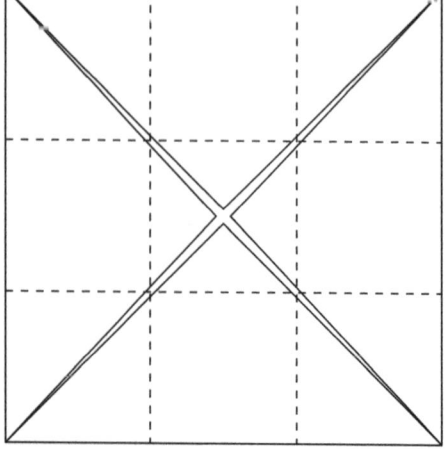

now fold it into thirds the other way

FIVE

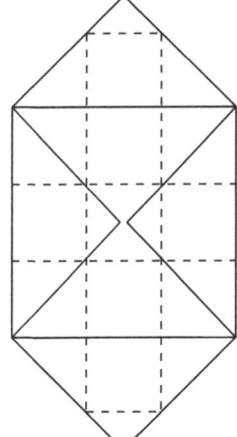

unfold the top and bottom flaps

SIX

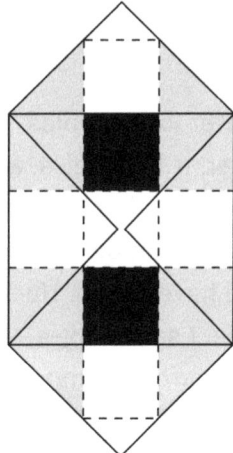

fold the shaded sections into the coloured-in sections

SEVEN

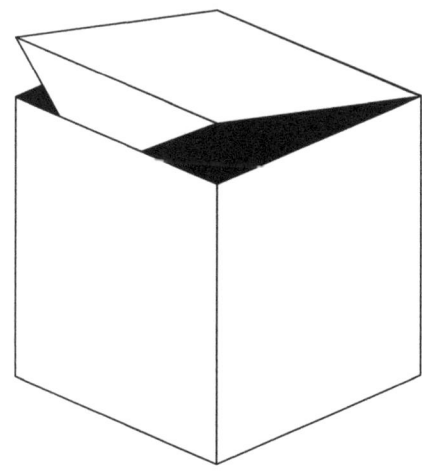

pinch the edges of your box to make
sure everything stays in place
close the lid and keep it that way

Jen Carter
—
from *Trinkets*

My daughter loves apples. Last week, after she was given one at school, she cradled it like a bird, a miracle, a seed like her. Pressing her nose against its skin, her thumbs stroked the smooth red peel, melting chestnut eyes aglow, as though it was the most precious treasure she could have found. Her gloved palms carried the apple our entire walk home. I sang ring-a-ring-a-roses as we went.

I find comfort in knowing she is a collector like me, and all the women in our family before us. Weathered books and gemstone slices, the plant my sister and I nurtured in secret, my grandmother's lipstick cases standing to attention. They are the trinkets that bring us comfort and hope. Today, that apple is all I can think about, as I am scuttling through the hospital grounds trying to find my mother.

The dread in my throat is treacly and sour, a familiar feeling now she has nearly died a few times, and I am growing used to the almosts. As the youngest of three sisters, I meet the stereotype of the littlest child in many ways: stubborn, emotional, and at this point in our adult lives, probably our mother's favourite. However, as the last one left at home when her health deteriorated, I became her carer, or keeper, and that baby-like, airy perspective on the world soon withered under the weight.

Now, my two older sisters follow closely behind me at a frantic pace, our feet hitting the vinyl of the floor in unison. *Clack, clack, clack.* This is the same hospital I was born in. Everywhere is baby-sick green, that warm-toned uncomfortable hue reserved only for run down, desperate spaces.

Weaving through the reception area, we work our way to the centre of the maze, towards the lifts to the higher floors.

We pile inside one of them without speaking. As we climb up, and other visitors and patients leave at their own floors, soon it is just us three, the mirror on the lift wall we are facing, and the three reflections staring back. Drained and used up versions of us, but still us. We are only seen together like this, this unit of three, when something bad happens.

In the last fifteen seconds it takes to reach our floor, I study my reflection. My hair is wispy and grown out, scooped back into a bun, and my already ghostly-pale complexion lends itself well to the reality of this. On usual days, *not your mam has had a stroke days*, the last thing I do before leaving the house is file through my features and match them to hers. I have so many of them. Our nose, oversized and slightly crooked, which we took from her Dad who passed before I was born. Our bulging eyes that always look scared, especially now, as I am staring into them in the mirror, swallowing back the sadness.

The atmosphere grows still as we get closer to the stroke ward, and I work hard to quieten my steps. The pattern we follow makes little sense, but I continue to lead my sisters down the corridors, following the signs, trying not to make contact with anyone else, at risk of looking lost. But we are, it's taking too long to find her, and my thoughts begin to deviate. Why does this keep happening? I am too young to be losing my only parent, surely, especially when I already have so little family alive.

Suddenly, there is a pull in my chest that feels familiar. I have been here before. The women I have known, either through stories or loving them in my own lifetime, their ghosts line the walls of this hospital. I plant my fidgeting hands firming in my coat pockets while they lead us to her, twirling the stalk of the imaginary apple in my hand.

***

A stale, aching fog follows us back to the car in silence. I am no longer in control of my body. I can see my joints like split pins, arms and legs swinging around in circles, but I have no say over their movements. My brother-in-law asks if we managed to get through to her. I don't attempt an answer.

'I guess we'll see,' my eldest sister replies while I shrink. Ten years on from the last time she almost died, here we are again. I am heavy and sick with grief.

As we drive over the River Tyne, I watch my history unfurl. The map rolls out, corner to corner, from my great grandmother born on Railway Terrace, Uncle David and John at the shipyards in Jarrow, to the sky over South Marine Park in all its topaz and silvers. I close my eyes and skim the riverbank, swirling lilacs and tubers, searching for signs of life. There must be something here to explain why, either young or tragically, the women in my family keep dying, and our pain is being passed down through the milk.

    I comb back through the generations in my mind until I find roots. I begin to wonder if it started with my great, great grandmother Louisa, the orphan, and the dog-eared bible she took to Alma House...

(

Agnieszka Szczotka

—

Occhio per Occhio

I spit on your palm and you slap my face. I like the impact of it, the instant wave of shock it sends through the body. It's a precision-requiring act. Compatibility check, if you wish. The palm needs to match the cheek, or the other way around. A wake-up call. Call to arms.

Between the passion and violence, the spit lands.

I arrived in Brescia from a dark city. A citadel of sadness (one might call it despair, though I admit this may sound a little dramatic and I aim to tread carefully to not be taken as such).

On my first evening I go out to eat. I am tired, as I woke up early and had gone to bed late, and after I am done with my food (*no vino no dolce no caffè*) the waiter brings me a glass of *limoncello* on the house. There's no questioning whether I might want one, just the assumption that I will. A hospitable yet uninvited act, one I find hard to refuse. After all, I am a guest here, in this house.

I take a sip. The sharp taste of lemon spills in my mouth, but the alcohol bites through the zest and I know I won't finish the glass. I scan the space for the bathroom and locate it and when the waiter goes to another room to serve *vino dolce e caffè* to more willing guests I pour the contents of the glass into my mouth, get up, and walk slowly towards the bathroom (as if not wanting to raise suspicions), where I spit the

)

liqueur into the sink. The yellowish substance snakes towards the hole, leaving a thick trail behind, before I rinse my mouth thoroughly multiple times.

But the alcohol lingers, burnt into the soft tissue of my mouth.

Between the passion and violence, the spit lands.

You spit in my mouth. Your spit is warm, and I find comfort in that, like sucking on a mother's breast, or falling asleep after a good fuck. And I wish I had asked you that day when my throat turned dry, and I couldn't get a word out.

> *You who switched me ON when I was OFF*
> *You who unmuted me when I was lost*
> *somnambulic in the lands with no words nor*
> *earthly delights because I pulled the short*
> *straw while floating in my mother's womb*

So, to compensate, I get on my knees and lick the wall well. Inch by inch, as if I was painting it with my tongue, coarse like a tongue of cat, I remove the layers of thick old paint and reveal the *frescos* hidden underneath.

It's a good career option, don't you all think? There are many *palazzos* in this city bathed in peach that might benefit from my foreign tongue licking their every hole, the wounds left behind by barbarians who invaded these lands years ago and covered the bodies that no longer are.

There are many ways of showing love. Painting frescos is one. Spitting is another.

Can I have a glass of water? I should have asked instead, to avoid the embarrassment.

Instead, I am given blood, because being a good Pole, martyrology keeps my heart alive. So we relate, I guess, in some sort of twisted way, but yours is joyous and mine is sad.

Between the passion and violence, a tiny red drop. Then – an open scar.

Last week in *Milano* I get on the metro for the first time in a while. It is hot and packed. I stand by the door trying to convince myself that the sudden proximity of strangers does not bother me – to distract myself I fix my gaze on the floor, my white trainers against the greyness of the linoleum. Then, a feeling of warmth around my nostrils. A tiny red drop stains the stitching around Nike's leather top. I lift my right hand and try to catch the blood in my palm *drip drip drip* while my left hand examines my pockets searching for tissues, or an old sock perhaps. At this point, anything goes. I find nothing, while the dripping intensifies. I make a boat from both my palms and try to catch the blood, but it is now a Sisyphean task.

My hands now stained and sticky as if I were eating red candyfloss, I let the blood drip, do its own thing and without lifting my head I wait I wait I wait

(*Veni vidi vici* it is not)

I wait patiently for someone to take notice while my white trainers turn red

> *Czerwone maki na Monte Cassino,*
> *Zamiast rosy piły polską krew.*
> *Po tych makach szedł żołnierz i ginął,*
> *Lecz od śmierci silniejszy był gniew*

until I find myself standing in a puddle of blood, and when my stop comes, I leave so quietly.

But before I go I pick up my demon from the floor who screams and kicks and spits blood so I say quietly *it's okay little one, it's okay… shhh, shhhh* I hold him in my arms like a mother holding a child like I hold a cat I cradle him with love I grab him by the neck so he won't scratch won't bite, and then he calms he calms he calms

while the voice says *occhio per occhio e pasta al dente.*

You are not your thoughts, someone once said. It might have been one of these resilience seminars we did back then. Who am I then, I ask myself while hearing voices in my head.

THIS VOICE IS ALL I HAVE

I can only feel the pain of my nipples being sucked dry and my ass getting cold from all the stones I sat on while I was on my way to the top (running up that hill).

I don't want to be resilient I want to be weak like a blade of grass weak and green so when the storm comes I don't break but flow.

I am a suckling sucking on the air, and starved of light I burned my face in the sun on the very first day I arrived, I am so fucking starved.

We will meet on the other side, says she who I met on the corner of the *piazza* where I sat frequently during the first week. Otherwise, what's the point?, she asks.

Between the passion and violence, the spit lands.

I find my fingernail cuttings on the desk. They are shaped like the cuts on the body of *Santa Giulia's*. (Even though she took more interest in her clit than climbing the walls she still liked to keep her nails clipped.)

)

Knock, knock… (silence) KNOCK, KNOCK! *Who's there?* I am searching for the clippers, Christ said after 40 days.

After three weeks in Italy my vaginal discharge turned into flour. In order to preserve it, I stop washing my underwear and buy 7 new pairs from H&M for the remaining days. I have a new ritual now – every evening I scrape the contents of each pair into the transparent, resealable bags I stole from the airports. I am methodical in my approach, careful not to waste, so once the scraping is done, I seal the contents of each bag, stick tape on it, and write the date with a black Sharpie.

Upon my return I will bake my own bread,
to make the transition easier.

The night before leaving she was sleepwalking again, and when she woke up, she found herself standing by the *Arengario* in *Piazza della Vittoria*. Without much hesitation she jumped the gate and walked up the stairs and then, as if touched by an angel or the holy trinity itself, the following incantation descended from her mouth:

Voi tutti Innocenti che amate to condividere la pizza
– pregate per noi
Voi che rompete gli spaghetti prima della cottura
– pregate per noi
Tutti voi Santi Profeti che bevete il cappuccio
dopo cena – pregate per noi

(

Miruna Fulgeanu

—

New Tattoo (Motivational Quote)

1.

Come home electric with intimacy, with this injury
       I paid for. *Love thy shoulder,* says the artist. Wash,

but only with the most scentless, virtuous soap.
       Touch, but only as you would a heat source. In the sun,

cover with fabric lightly, as if shielding an animal
       breathing, breathing. At home, the body feels enlightened;

it has learnt about the body. Now when I want to read it,
       I place a mirror behind me, into which I look through

the mirror in front — then, after dusk, I move   )
       about the house shirtless like a boy.

2.

My better judgement
is always growing heads —
large violet heads
of an alarmingly *better* better judgement.
Together we fine-dine
on every new belief I make.
I didn't know how else to keep this one alive.

3.

In the middle of my enlightenment, I was set back by a dream in which Man had made a burrow for himself at the bottom of my garden. It made sense that in the dream I lived in a 17th-century castle, while he had been abandoned by his friends & admirers alike. Without my knowledge, but in complicity with Handsome Gardener, he had been feeding off my scraps for months. I decided to be merciful and let him stay. Though if I'm honest, this was only because his total downfall made me feel like I had won.

Slowly, I felt myself giving over to the anxiety that Man's downfall was merely a tactic. I started to worry that he was lying in wait for the day when I might go down to the garden, to check on the azaleas or the pheasant pen. Or the day when Groundsman might forget to lock my door. And suddenly I found I had become defenceless in my own home...

(The next day, I sat myself down between the mirrors. I was there for hours. Every time I felt shame, I read the words and counted them, how their motivation extended into the distance.

4.

Here, I have done	the violence
myself,	and to myself.
I have a lot of	swords and
pomades.	Now I will
look after myself	*so well*
for 2–4 weeks,	depending on
weather conditions	skin type
determination	moisturising abilities.
Most likely I'll just	do 3,
I can't wait	or want, or need
instructions can't want instructions anymore.	

)

Rozie Kelly

—

from *Salt Tooth*

Our bodies are the texts that carry the memories
and therefore remembering is no less than reincarnation.
      Katie Cannon

Do not, however, make the mistake of thinking that all desire is yearning.
      Maggie Nelson

Suppose I were to tell you that I was complicit? Let's begin there.

I am watching my breath on the window, and I am aching for the lack of breath on my neck. I am watching my breath on the window, and it is mingling with the smoke from the roll-ups I no longer inhale. Do you know what it is like to be addicted to intimacy? We all do, I suppose. We know the feeling of fingers tiptoeing across one another, finding the way to slip into one another, to cross over one another, that first time. Not the first time you hold hands, not necessarily, but the first time your hands do it without asking your permission. I won't say the word because that's not what I am talking about. I am talking about necks. About forearms and the certain twist of a blue vein. I am talking about one particular freckle, a bead of sweat, the base of the spine pulling inwards.

Men have no idea about pain. They think they do but they don't. Tenderness is a word weighted with meaning. We are decimated with it. We are hammered down with it, reconfigured, reformed. We reform ourselves on its behalf. I blow smoke against the window; it spreads out in a sheet. Action and reaction. It is raining outside, and it is the kind of rain that feels angry. I pull the window closed a little more – I can see my breath on the glass and in the air. It is spring, but it's the part of spring that is also winter. On my kitchen counter there is the rolling tobacco that I don't smoke anymore, and there is a glass of wine. It's a glass that you bought for me, from a charity shop. Absentmindedly, having forgotten my birthday. The glass is green and warped and I love it all the more for its transience. There are two green glasses and one purple one. The purple lives on the shelf, most of the time. I drink from the green ones. The ones we used to use. We never went to France, but France is all over you. It's in your hair and your fingers and that navy blue jumper of yours.

We met when we were young. We weren't, really. Not in the literal sense. But I was naïve. *Tender.* I was not fully formed, despite being well into my thirties. You are an old soul, as they say. You've been here before. You have a hard shell that I could not crack with my weak and splintering fingernails. You were a little older than me, in years. You were young in that way we allow men to be. A twinkle. A sock on the floor of a bedroom, just feet from a hamper. Crumbs on a sideboard. A coffee ring on an old wooden table. You were older than me and younger than me and you were forgiven. I bent myself into abstract shapes, and I will never forgive myself.

When I rub my finger and thumb together, sometimes I can still feel you there. I have thought of you often and every which way, but mostly I do so from this spot by the kitchen window. I have watched the weather follow its entire cycle since we began. Now it is spring again and I'm not sure I believe the evidence of life around me. The landscape of winter felt more honest. At least the wind still cuts me a little. I do not know how I will cope with warm sunlight without weeping.

I will tell the story from my kitchen window and watch it play out in the reflections on the glass.

I am putting on a play. When we met, and we were young and we were old and we didn't know better, you circled me like a fox. Can you believe I didn't realise your eyes were green until after it was done? What an extraordinary lack of attention. Your eyes were red, they were black, they were shaded, they were clear. From the side they were grey. Only afterwards could I see that your irises were green. You have eyes that should have belonged to a fictional princess. They do not make sense wrapped in gently creased lids, ruddy cheeks, thick eyebrows. They project an innocence you have no right to.

When we met, I was working a job that I hated, and I was tired. My skin was sallow, and I was thin. You looked at me like I would make a delicious snack and for once I felt like someone who could fit between meals.
I watched you warily, I kept my back to the wall for a little while. I think now, looking back, this delighted you. Eventually, when you asked me out, I was so surprised that I said yes. I was supposed to know you in a professional capacity, you were a client at the job I hated. But that was the beginning of it all. That was when I changed everything. I quit that job and I signed on at the Jobcentre with its stained carpets and empty smell and I started taking baths rather than showering and I rubbed coconut oil into my hair and my feet.

For our first date you took me to the cinema. I can see us walking there in light rain, me concerned with my hair getting wet, preoccupied by *control.* You, dancing. You danced with your words, you danced with your hands. You are dancing across my windowpane. I draw a line in the condensation, and you follow it, pulling me along by my scarf, making me laugh despite myself. You have a conspiratorial energy, always. You make people feel like you're sharing a secret with them, even when you're just buying a newspaper. You dare people to laugh with you.
    We watched a terrible film. I had been expecting something arty and pretentious. Then I would be right about you, and I could go to bed satisfied. But instead, we saw Lara Croft. The new one, not the Jolie one. You told me I looked like her and I ignored the obscene flattery and instead imagined how it would feel to be able to do pull-ups. Imagined what it might be like to be strong. To live without the definite knowledge of inevitable defeat. We didn't hold hands that night, but you did slide one of yours up my sleeve so that the callouses on your palm grazed my knuckles. You took my wrist, just a little bit too tight. You moved me where you wanted me, and I obeyed.

The thing I liked about you was that you made me fall in love with everything around me. You handed me your sea-glass vision and I gazed about, astounded. Wasn't it all soft? Wasn't the world kind? At this moment, as I stare out of my kitchen window, it is hailing. There is thunder and the hail is hard and heavy, and a large tomcat is walking across the lawn. He moves as if he cannot feel the hail hitting him, and perhaps he cannot. I project you onto every animal I see. He has red hair like yours.

I cannot sit by this window forever. I know this, although my life does little to prove it to me. Aside from bathroom breaks, I do it in shifts. I do my best to order in supplies. I am not ready for spring. My cocoon is rotten inside, where there should be wings there are just bones.

I didn't hear from you for an entire week after that night at the cinema. Seven whole days, after all those months when every time I turned my head there you were. I imagined you selling heroin on the street. The first hit is always free. That's how they get you. Of course, you wouldn't have been doing that. You'd have been in London, most likely, doing something important that involved wearing a cashmere scarf and having a lunch meeting. Interviewing someone significant I'd not heard of. The result is the same. During those seven days I cried a lot, although I think I was quite happy. I went to the Jobcentre and lied about trying to find work. I cleaned my kitchen with an extremely small square of sponge. By the time you phoned me I was wary again. The very fact that you phoned me, rather than texting like everybody else does, threw me. I swayed from side to side with the phone cold against my ear.

    I'm on the train, you said. I'm imagining that the rapeseed is out and that everything is yellow. Can you see it?

    Yes, I said. I can see it.

    You told me afterwards that you'd already decided, then, what was going to happen between us. I believe you now.

I'd *love* to introduce you to my friends, you said. At the time I took it as a compliment, a statement of impossibility, a regretful one. It wasn't until afterwards that it occurred to me that if you wanted to then you could have. I wanted you to introduce me to your friends. I wanted to see the jealousy in their gaze, and the pride in yours. Look what I have here – your green eyes would say. Isn't she a sweet thing, my little lovebird? I introduced you to my friends and they cocked their heads to one side.

When you stop working the days stop meaning. People joke about daytime TV, but I often just find myself in different rooms, sat quietly and not thinking at all. I eat breakfast for every meal like I'm desperate to start again. I am desperate to start again, but I am also prone to drama, as my mum would say. I do leave the window. I do leave the house. I do work, a bit, although that's all on the laptop now. I see a therapist. I must be doing better because Mum doesn't call me every day, she doesn't sound out of breath when she speaks to me. I wouldn't say I feel better, not exactly. I feel cleaner, like I've done an efficient job of hollowing the feelings from inside of me. Slopping them into a bowl on a table for a professional to tease through. Guts and seeds. Let's make a soup with this, I imagine her saying. We mustn't waste anything. I am better and I am worse, but that has nothing to do with you anymore. You are gonney-gone-gone.

We went for dinner, after you returned from those silent seven days, after you called me from the train. You behaved as if it was completely normal not to talk for that long after a date. You behaved as if you didn't know I would have been questioning your hand on my wrist, the zip of my jeans, the wall behind the cinema brushing my cheek. The moss pushing between my fingers. Questioning my implicit loss in value against your explicit gain. You behaved as if it was normal, so I decided to believe it was. I began to fuck you in public places. Bathrooms and woodland and alleys. And when you went silent afterwards, I flagellated myself with that silence. I dominated myself on your behalf. I was the ultimate enactment of submission. I think that delighted you, too. Men want to feel powerful, after all. Especially the ones who already are.

*

I am a good woman. There are daffodils dancing outside my window, just like you liked to dance. Your taste in music is terrible, it made me wince. But oh, how you loved to dance. I think it was how you saw yourself, how you imagined your character would behave in a movie. He would take the hand of the prettiest girl, lead her to the middle of the floor. All eyes on him, but through the prism of watching her. She is a crystal, an object of power, a focus of energy. You are the magician teasing the magic from her. Feeding berries to a fawn – no sudden movements, you might frighten her. The crowds watch as you spin her around and her dress swirls around her smooth, thin legs. Everybody envies you. I see your face in the window, pressed into her shoulder as the music slows. You look so *satisfied*. You are selfish in your happiness. You gobble it all up, yum yum yum.

    I fast and I waste and I bend and I become yet more pliable. I will never be as shy as a fawn; I will never be as thin and graceful as the women on screen. I am a good woman. You put your thumb in my mouth and called me a good girl.

Soon we were dating. We held hands in the street, although we had not yet done so without it being deliberate. You met my mother and she loved you, which is always a terrible sign. But I mustn't get ahead of myself. Before the fucking but after the cinema, there was dinner. I was deeply uncomfortable that day. I curled in my seat; I regretted my outfit. I kept shuffling away from you on the leather banquette we shared. I couldn't bear you having all this access to my face in profile, I needed to look at you head on if I was to have a chance. We ate steak and stuffed potato skins and New York cheesecake. The thick textures of the food began to soften my edges. As my stomach strained, I relaxed. I twisted to face you in my seat. I pulled one leg up beside me and folded my arms. I've never seen you look so happy.

    Yes? you said. You waited expectantly.

    I missed you, I said.

    I know you did, you replied.

The phone rings. I have done very little this morning. I showered and washed my hair, which felt like the most extraordinary amount of effort for very little reward. My hair lies lank on my shoulders. I consider cutting it all off. Perhaps it is time for me to change who I am again.

    Charlotte? she says, as if she didn't ring the right number.

    Mum.

    Oh good… I wasn't sure if you would answer.

    She's breathless again.

    Why wouldn't I answer?

    Oh, I don't know. I just had this *feeling*.

Mum has always had these *feelings*, as long as I can remember. Sometimes they are innocuous, as today's seems to be. But once she moved us to a completely new town based on one of these unexplained urges. *We're animals, Char,* she'd say to me. *We have ancient instincts that we've learned to ignore.* I don't want to live in ignorance. I never quite forgave her for that move. It was the first time in my life that I'd made a friend, a good one, and I was forced to give her up. My friend had cream carpets in her house and her mother spoke in soft tones and all her Barbies had matching outfits. Their furniture was bleached pine and you had to take your shoes off at the door and her mum fed me salmon. When I went for a sleepover, she let me use one of the guest towels, fluffy and warm from the tumble drier. It was a lot to lose.

Well, I'm fine. I've answered the phone. What's up?

Just checking in. It's been exactly nine weeks today, so I thought it was best to make sure you're not doing anything stupid.

I don't think it's useful to remind me of things like that, you know, Mum. I can't imagine Dr Phillips would think that's a good idea.

Well, she doesn't know everything.

She knows more than you.

I didn't call for this attitude. Have you eaten?

Yes (I hadn't)

Taken your meds?

Yes (I actually had, but I'd forgotten for the previous four days so who knows what good it was doing me).

Right. Well. Take care then love.

Bye Mum...

I held the phone to my face and waited for the line to go dead. It would take a while, I knew, as Mum would be doing the same. I think this was how we expressed love for one another, this silent vigil. Each waiting for the other to give up. She always gives up first. I can see her in the glass, the skin pinched between her eyes, the hand not holding the phone shaking, the tremors so a part of her that she's managing to put together a cigarette one handed, compensating for the vibrations, her mouth pursed. I think you liked my mother. I could never tell whether it was patronising, or whether it was because it annoyed me, or just because you were endlessly fascinated by people, all of them, but you'd sit with her for hours, refilling the Pernod that she insisted on drinking, topping up her small water jug, letting her tell you about astrology and the benefit system and UFOs and her *feelings*.

Intimacy took us a long time. The physical was fine. I just gave myself over to that, I didn't need to be vulnerable to be used. But anything resembling a real connection would make me balk. For all your faults, you were always open to connection. If you looked in my eyes for too long, I'd look away, make a joke, or occasionally get irrationally angry with you, out of nowhere. Your green eyes sought mine for a long time, and if we were dressed, I'd behave as if naked in public, rushing to cover myself and my shame. When we were physical it was different, but then it always is, isn't it? Is there anyone in the world that's truly themselves when they're fucking someone? I doubt it. You're measuring personas against one another. Who is masculine, who is feminine, and to what extent? How well are we playing our roles? How believable are we? I am very believable; I know that much. It's something about the eyes. Looking like a doe can be very useful sometimes. Submissive by association. I look like I need help. I look like I couldn't hurt a fly. You know differently now, don't you? And I do too, I suppose.

)

Louis Bailey

—

from *The Night Run*

Dusk

<u>The Watchman's Rattle</u>

The dots and dashes of dusk
code this flying toad
in oak and murmur.

dididi

In the gloaming
this mottled face of stone
rattles two-tone.

(*didididahdahdah*

Static, charged at the crepuscular.
This ferny owl churns
corpse fowl —
a goat-sucker turned
puckeridge.

didididahdahdahdididit

In the limbo of light
this nighthawk stalks moth-time
becomes reclusive
a stalled transmission
reduced to click, reduced to flicker:
bird, lizard, bark.

I'm running along an old disused railway line in the Longdendale Valley, Derbyshire, on a midsummer's night. The route follows a series of reservoirs which feed the nearby cities of Manchester and Salford, and forms part of the long-distance Trans Pennine Trail.

Bored of the gravel path and needing a change of pace, I decide to cut through a field onto the open moors. It's my first run in the hills since surgery. Weeks of being immobilised and housebound have made jelly of my limbs. I've missed not being able to get out and struggled with the enforced bed rest. My legs are stiff and my hands jut out awkwardly, willing my body forward with each downturned fist. For the last little while, my arms have been pinned to my side, leaving me looking and feeling like a cardboard marionette, and unable to stretch or lift anything heavier than a tea cup. Instead, in the fashion of a Victorian consumptive, I've been swaddled in bandages and gauze with a drain bag either side, the tubing suckled to each armpit like a leech.

I reach the edge of the moor just as the sun is setting. Emboldened by the enveloping darkness, I take my shirt off and reveal my newly-healed chest for the first time. The sutures are still visible; little snatches of cotton peer out from underneath each nipple, which have been stitched and pulled tight like a purse. My running slows to a jog and I follow the sound of a cuckoo to a clump of trees. I am just about to emerge out of the woodland when I hear it – a gentle rumble coming from behind me. I do an about-turn and retrace my steps to the small clearing below.

The rumbling starts up again. Low-pitched and guttural yet also robotic and slightly out of range, between notes, between places, and somehow not of this realm. The sun intensifies, the golden glow of magic hour scorching the ground. The day explodes into a kaleidoscope of colours – an ombré of blue, purple, grey, orange – a swirl of sacred soup and a final burst before the ushering in of the night. But, before that, dusk – that twilight place where the last of the light makes silhouettes of the silent things. There is a calmness to this place; it is a space of revelation, of gentle slumber for some, and slow awakening for others. The starkness of the day begins to lose its edges and my ego – in all its pride, fragility, centricity – is offered up in sacrifice to the more-than-human world.

didididahdahdah

The rumbling continues. Persistent, dissonant, mechanical. I've never heard this sound before, and don't have anything lofty to compare it to – just the slow grind of metal upon metal, the creak of an old door. It sounds like an elliptical, a verbal tic, a thoughtful pause – throaty and expectant. My mind attempts to fill the spaces left by the limits of what I think I can see and hear. It sounds like a stalled transmission; no, a reaching out, unable to connect. It isn't a loud sound yet it somehow manages to permeate the woods and the still summertime air. It has a ventriloquist's flair for misdirection.

    I manage to pinpoint the sound to a single tree and so I sit at the base of it, mesmerised. It is now dark. I sense movement and look up but can't decipher what I am looking at: Bird? Lizard? A piece of fern or bark? Scratching and shadows. I feel like I've lost my senses. If only, like a telegraph operator, I could translate its signal – the dots and dashes of Morse code, the urgency of its call. I imagine it in human form, shapeshifting into a huddle of throat singers summoning spirits or taming wild animals into deep sleep. It is later that I learn its name.

*

Nightjars: tricksy and enigmatic creatures of myth. In the beginning, before they were seen, they were goatsuckers, pillagers of milk, spreaders of disease. They were the souls of unbaptised children, forgotten and doomed to wander the world for eternity. They were an abomination, a cackle of witches lurking in the bushes. Villagers were scared of what lay beyond the boundary wall, of the flickered figures outside the confines of the church. But they were also fascinated by these cryptic souls – these elusive licks of light, these strange beasts of eerie call. These birds spoke of the shadows, hinted at a world never ventured – arriving silently before the shroud of darkness and leaving before first light.

    Folklore casts the nightjar as deceptive and untrustworthy, the embodiment of all that is unholy. In early rural beliefs around the world, nightjars were thought to be harbingers of doom; were said to be thieves who stole milk directly from the udders of cattle, inducing pestilence and famine. Nightjars were scapegoated for society's ills, became vessels for man's failures and fears.

The earliest accusations levied at the nightjar can be traced to the fourth century B.C. and the writings of Aristotle who claimed that: 'Flying upon the goat, it sucks them, whence it has its name. They say that when it has sucked the teat it becomes dry, and that the goat becomes blind.' 'Puckeridge', as it was termed, was caused not by the plucking of nightjars but by warble flies laying eggs under the skin of young calves. And yet, even after the declaration of this fact, naturalists were still forced to come to the nightjar's defence well into the eighteenth and nineteenth centuries. In *The Natural History of Selbourne* (1789), English naturalist Gilbert White claims: 'It is the hardest thing in the world to shake off superstitious prejudices: they are sucked in as it were with our mother's milk.'

*

When I started my gender transition back in the early 2000s, there was very little visibility or general awareness about trans people. I was in my early twenties and knew that I didn't identify as a woman and had never felt female despite that being the marker that was assigned to me at birth. I didn't yet know that there was a term for how I felt, or that there were words available for what I was moving towards. I scoured the libraries of Brighton – where I was living as a student at the time – for information, but only found brief mentions of something called transsexualism in a handful of medical textbooks. Transsexualism: the word sounded so cold and off-putting. I didn't relate to the concept of being in the wrong body. I wasn't in the wrong body. This was my body, and as much as there were adjustments that were needed to make it a home – hair growth here, muscle growth there – there was much about it that I had grown to like. The framing and language of trans identities back then felt so formal and 'othering'.

It was around this time that I heard about a club in London which ran regular drag king shows: Club Wotever. I had heard of drag queens – Brighton was glittered with them – but drag *kings*? So began the once-a-month pilgrimage to London in search of friendship and self-knowledge. Within a few months, I had created an alter-ego called Lord Louie and was touring him around queer clubs in London and the South East. Lord Louie Englebert Humpadinck was a debauched, Eton-educated socialite who was squandering his inheritance on extravagant parties, filling the family manor with exquisitely designed Greco-Roman replicas, endowed with larger-than-life genitalia and posteriors, and busts dripping with rare and precious gemstones, metals and animal skins. With youthful self-righteousness, I intended my performances to be an urgent and necessary wake-up call to Britain's class system, a satire of the one per cent elite, a performative manifesto about the ever-growing gap between rich and poor. But my performances never really got very far in getting the point across. The chaotic nature of queer cabaret in combination with my own method of drinking to excess out of pre-performance nerves meant that, more often than not, by the time I got on stage I was so drunk I could barely remember how to dance the Charleston let alone follow through with my manifesto with any real wit. But I had a good time, and those precious nights out helped me find community and a growing queer consciousness.

Over the coming months, I would be performing less and less but inhabiting the guise of Louie more and more. I started binding my chest each morning before getting dressed. Initially, I used bandages but later bought a binder. I sacrificed comfort for a more streamlined appearance and liked the new-found flatness of my chest. Soon, I was donning fake facial hair, and would snip off the ends of my already short hair to glue to my cheeks and chin – a soul patch here, moustache and sideburns there. What started as a monthly performance seeped into the everyday and, over time, would become a second skin.

For the first time in my life, I felt that there were moments where my gender was seen, but there was a catch: if I was recognised as male – which occurred about half of the time – then people read me as a pre-pubescent or adolescent boy, not a young adult in their early twenties. And as soon as I spoke, the pitch of my voice immediately coded me as female. I grew frustrated with not having the fullness of my identity recognised and was exhausted by the uncertainty of not knowing how my gender (and my age) would be 'read'. While initially my gender disruptions were a cause of great defiance and joy, over time they felt restrictive. I yearned for a deep voice and a more masculine body, yearned for my gender to feel less performative and more embodied.

My first dose of testosterone changed everything. It was the largest needle I had ever seen, and as the nurse plunged it deep into the upper quadrant of my right buttock, I felt instant relief. Those bi-weekly shots thrust me deep into a second puberty and marked the beginning of my medicalised transition away from female. But my trajectory was still unknown. It would take time for new secondary sex characteristics to mark themselves on my body, and for a new mind–body connection to grow. I was stepping through a funfair mirror into a whole new reality of being, and being seen, in the world. I was twenty-five and overwhelmed with the intensity of the experience and the reactions that my transition was eliciting from family, friends, colleagues and strangers. The sheer joy that I felt was tempered by the fear and anxiety from family that I was 'ruining my life' and would be 'shunned by society' for what I had done. It was a difficult time, and the noise was too much.

*

Notoriously reclusive, some ornithologists believe that it is entirely possible that various sub-species of nightjar have evolved so as to be invisible to the human eye. These deep-stealth creatures are so well camouflaged they have managed to evade human detection altogether. This begs the question: if we can't see them then how do we know they exist?

Certain species are only believed to have existed due to partial remains that have been found. The Vaurie's nightjar (*Caprimulgus centralasicus*) is known from a single dead bird collected in September 1929 in Xinjiang, north-western China.[1] Despite extensive surveys and searches, it has never been found, dead or alive, since.[2] And we know about the Nechisar nightjar (*Caprimulgus solala*) due to the existence of a single wing and a handful of battered tail feathers scraped off a dusty road by a team of scientists in 1990 in the Gamo Gofa province of Ethiopia, the product of roadkill. There was a possible sighting of

---

1. The specimen – held at the Natural History Museum in Tring, UK – was initially thought to be that of an adult female, but recent investigations suggest that it might actually be that of a juvenile. See M. Schweizer, C. Etzbauer, H. Shirihai et al., 'A molecular analysis of the mysterious Vaurie's Nightjar *Caprimulgus centralasicus* yields fresh insight into its taxonomic status', in *Journal of Ornithology* (2020), pp. 161, 635–50.
2. H.D. Jackson, 'A review of the evidence for the translocation of eggs and young by nightjars (*Caprimulgidae*)', in *Ostrich: Journal of African Ornithology*, 78/3 (2007), pp. 561–72.

the Nechisar nightjar in 2009 by bird enthusiasts but no evidence collected, and despite extensive surveys, a 2015 scientific field trip found no evidence of its existence. In the absence of definitive proof either way, these birds currently exist in duality – simultaneously dead and alive, real and unreal.

The scientific status of nightjars is itself under dispute and it is not known whether certain sub-species of nightjar, because of their elusiveness and powers to evade human detection, are rare, extinct or locally common. Perhaps the Vaurie's nightjar and the Nechisar have managed to evolve in such a way to make it difficult or impossible to be seen by humans and continue to fly undetected, only to be seen by other nightjars. And, if so, are there other animals that exist which remain invisible to us, which have successfully eluded the human clutch?

That these nightjars – and potentially other species – have existed (exist?) but have never knowingly been seen alive, haunts me. I am awed by their superpowers, how they fill the space between fact and imagination. In the absence of live recordings, in the absence of the real thing, what creatures can we conjure into being?

(

*

I had initially wanted two of them – a bird either side in the style of the traditional swallow tattoos that adorn the necks and chests of sailors – but the tattooist recommended having just one bird. She placed the stencil over my chest: an almost life-sized nightjar perched on my sternum, its wings reaching up over my shoulders and tail feathers extending down over my ribs. *Like it's protecting your heart.* It took around fifteen hours for the bird to come to life.

The pain was bearable for the most part. Things got pinchy as the needle dragged over my collar bone and vibrated across my torso. A white hotness snagged the scars that encircled each nipple, shiny from healing but still lumpy to the touch. The tattooist transformed my chest from site of surgery to place of hatching, making twigs of my ribs and padding the nest with insects and foliage. She did everything she could to make my skin appealing to this elusive bird. Then I waited.

A bird appears. Its large dark eye peers over my left nipple, its whiskered beak twitching towards my armpit, in search of prey. A swallow-tailed moth elegantly perches on my shoulder, just out of reach. The delicate plumage of the nightjar mingles with the wispy, dark patches of hair that graze my chest. I've been on testosterone for over a decade now and can still only muster a few strands of growth. But the nightjar doesn't judge. It stretches out languidly around the angular curves of my chest and purrs in approval at its new home.

The stealthy markings of the nightjar are an example of disruptive patterning — a form of evolutionary camouflage developed and refined over millennia to help protect certain species from predation. It works to conceal the nightjar by employing certain colours and patterns which work to break up the bird's outline, hindering detection. As a result, the bird blends into its environment, its form disguised through clever combinations of colour, texture and patterning — specs of dusty grey, strips of mottled oak, cryptic details which unfold outwards into the surrounding terrain; streaked and barred over wood, earth and air, unfurling out of view. It is the ultimate conjuring trick, designed to baffle and confuse a curious or predatory gaze. It takes a flicker of movement, the blink of an eye, for the form to be coaxed back into visibility. Like looking at a Magic Eye picture, the skill lies in patience, knowing where to look, and looking through the landscape. Glimpses of this enigmatic bird can be fleeting, and the subtlest changes in atmosphere and light can mean that the nightjar might disappear again before our very eyes.

For the nightjar, concealment is reliant upon the obliteration of form. For me, transition enabled me to overcome the limits of my bodily form, allowed me to stretch into the spaces beyond the confines of my birth sex, and societal expectations of me growing up as a girl. It gifted me the opportunity to obliterate previous incarnations of my identity and embody a new blueprint of gender. Just as the nightjar faces the sun in an attempt to conceal their shadow, so I try my best to hide all evidence that I was ever read as female. My legal gender has been recognised as male for some time now, with my passport stamped and all boxes ticked accordingly.

But that is only half the story.

Dominic J. Jaeckle
—
A Flower for Laura Lee Burroughs (Magnolia or Redbud)*

(

—
*   In the late 1930s, The Coca-Cola Company aimed to spearhead a campaign to better establish their product as a household staple and enrapture the middle-class homemaker's market. A Trojan horse, the resulting promotion was run through the distribution of a ¢10 mail-order publication on flower arrangement. Three illustrated editions, authored by St. Louis resident Laura Lee Burroughs, that would explore the practice of domestic and decorative horticulture as a means of sitting a bottle side-by-side with a bouquet: *Flower Arranging: A Fascinating Hobby* (Vols. I and II), and *Homes and Flowers: Refreshing Arrangements*. In 1940, the first of Burroughs' works was offered to the public to a thunderous reception. More than a million and a half copies were printed to meet the degree of demand, and a second and third volume would follow in 1941 and 1942. Following the first outdoor wall advertisement for Coca-Cola – a hand-painted sign in Cartersville, Georgia, 1894 – the replacement of the spring-sealed Hutchinson bottle with the signature hobble-skirt design of 1915, and the company's fiftieth anniversary celebrations, 1935, the campaign cemented Coca-Cola's market centrality and inflamed its suburban appeal. Mother of author William S. Burroughs, Laura Lee's work sits in poetic counterpoint to her son's subsequent experiments with collage and cut-up – a formal flower arrangement of his own – and the following poem mimics the Burroughs brand of *découpé* by borrowing words and phrases pooled exclusively from Laura Lee's three publications for Coca-Cola to essay a basis from which to build an afterwork out of the family habit. 'Magnolia or Redbud' was first exhibited as a commissioned installation work in the St. Louis Lambert International Airport (St. Louis, Missouri) – September 2021 until March 2022 – with thanks to Marianne Laury and Paul Artspace.

I.

You set the table for dinner and
—joining the ranks of the so-called
modern flowers
and water-loving animals—
        know that your interest needs
break the line

Needs make up for other kinds of deficiency

                                                  So, you leave

You search the garden for sunken things

For magnolia or redbud
        or a second piece of fruit—

)

for treasured and numbered heirlooms
and conversations that'll adorn the room

Like severed ends in vinegar
        —deep water
or four feet of snow

The leaves that you had overlooked—
whilst the indianhead blooms,
they flourish and multiply everywhere now

—becoming stalwart composites
        (like American Pewter or a number
of museums throughout
                the country)

Dominic J. Jaeckle

(

II.

But here, the apparent centre of our interest
is something else

Penetrating the motif
is a little garden saint, as you imagine it
    —sufficiently decorative alone
it moves things like the weather

Apparently effective but inexpensive, it spikes like Florida, the saint

Scrolling book or tablecloth

We look to the saint, and we are expecting a flat surface—
    no desert—
no vagabond *objet d'art*—
    but something stable   )
and find only a dark centre, a wind
of interest dappled like light through ice

Everything radiates according to inclination and form
    & so you move
only to mock the orange blossoms and white doves (*hard work*)
and find your ideas all repeated in the fauna and in birds

(those that form a *We* set in deep chestnut orange
    everlastings, nicotiana and cosmos)

III.

You remember
last winter, in an uncovered garden
where you realised that hollyhocks are not as dependable as cut flowers

& you think of Magnolia and Redbud, again

But now, as the idea rises,
You know you need leave the rest for the birds
& as decoration without cost you relate pictures and forms
      Recalling that
around eighteen hundred and sixty an
        art flourished in England and America called
                              skeletonising

(

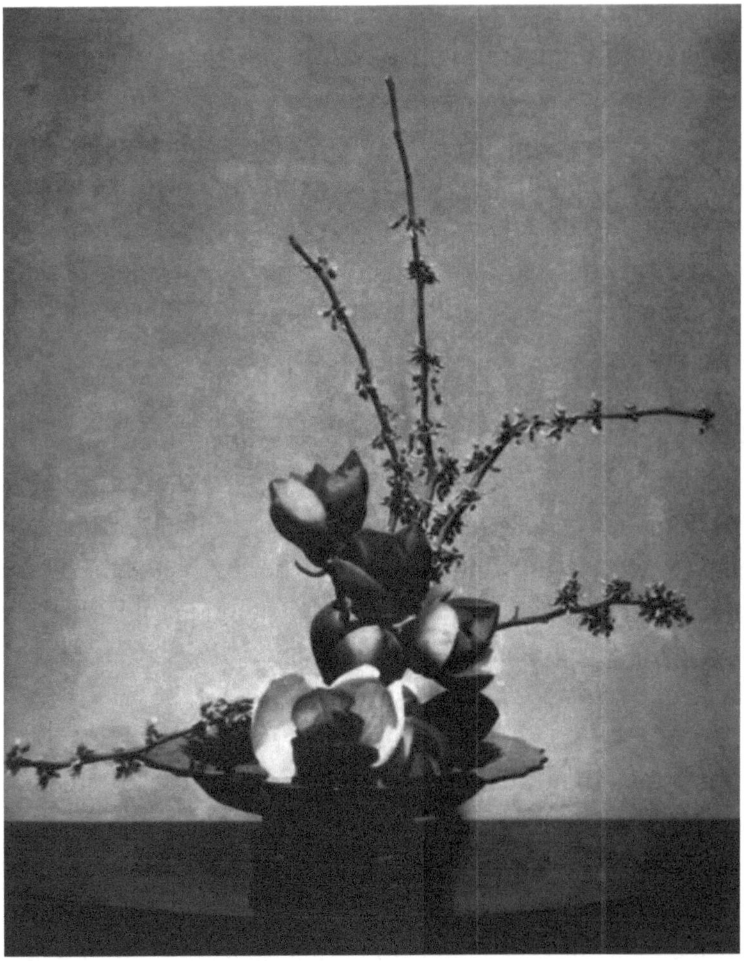

)

Aria Hughes-Liebling

—

from *The Lesser Mysteries*

They say they will dock here. That I will see a large river. They are dogs, fully wooden. They are things done, things shown, things said.

Long ago, where long ago was. A commentary to dogs wandering, as men walking through long rooms—who show themselves through a disregarded half-sweat. Who permeate not a trophy, but a reminder. And in snippets—depicted how. A currency of shapely bottles and shapely territory lines. Traded between estimated margins as though promises would be condoned as kept. Or at least made smaller, then larger—a greater content, meant in comparison or by sight. Something plated or something nearer to a downed bat.

This was mostly a flooded place—its own moribund or winking defect. A lint-lined or limestone-weighted piety—so cold in those watery places. Like an admitted, but unused nook—waiting for fellow countrymen and a rewarded popularity. Is a deep corner—corresponding with anyone crouching, teasing. Or any figure carrying ichor in their veins. A nook which is scarcely infatuated yet is observed clamoring for attention again and again. An agreement eventually indulged—with some enthusiasm and to no end.

There was rain, then violence—an archive sown across earlier calendars and inevitably concealed. The texture of an immature infant—maybe decrepit, left alone in slabs. Who pebbled the camps with tall cries and gave the stone needed for construction—laying down arenas rutted with pestilence and shapes too broad to be law. But law sprouted anyway. Was rounded out and renounced. Was mentioned to be vast—written, then detailed with a single hackle raised along its back.

Doctors were called to treat the law's hackle—the first sign of a greater disease. They examined the law's tongue and its reflex but were stopped by a tunneling sum. Something bulbous running along each stroke of wind. People went naked—waiting for cloth and food.

And those who didn't want these comforts laughed at the doctor's naivety—themselves trapped by that same bulbous air.

 Their likeness was proven and a cliff's earth pressed limbs upon the scene—its missing weight fumbling until the coastline was pockmarked. How empty depressions, like those of an already dead animal, acted as an alert for the townspeople—who did not search for it. A long praise, like the mention of a ground that was run-in.

 Anything afterward was inconsequential. Was refused entry or sustenance. And drew only cold air. The delayed mockery from those dying—misplaced—moving from one hand to the other. Right to left or otherwise directionless. And made from baskets of tired mirror—an object skimmed from lesser questions and mangled into riddle.

 Regardless, domestic scenes became increasingly frequent. Each a dog, their significance remaining unaltered. A modernly beak made to soothe a poor throw. She is—such a red baby. And the home— ecstatic.   )

 Averse to warm bets, the family guts its breakfast. They are chapped and lenient with the food. Handshook in appearance. A sparse or possibly unfortunate, small to dismal to gradually hollowing movement—an arch to surrounding hills. The things nearly called birds. Humming to hide the table's value.

 The watchmaker, like others, parsed out his losses as an initiation— leaving scraps of clothing to his home and children. The butcher, the mayor, the shopkeeper also plotted fairly. Staged themselves upon peppered horns. Men sprawled together—ears in buckets. The children become adults and sell the buckets. Money enough for a shorthand of passage.

 Reverence followed in suites of sturdy moss—was regularly accepted and then pushed into the ground. Giving us hills and ultimately summits—shrinking our lakes and dilating homes. More and more dejected courts resembling dejected wives from good marriages or a

fantasy of mires fenced by drought. How our guilt eventually churned
and created a storm—unearthing ourselves to a lesser morning.

    Three felt lucky that morning—went west and found oil, gold
and stone. Winners—hugged by sense, but kept peck-fed and guilted
into ringing. A splintered fenland now grown to cut grain. To build
homes that were deciduous by angles—a lean nature frantic to lie
by fault.

    I began sleeping more formally with no loss of consciousness
or difference between morning and undressing. Consistent hours,
where I awoke in the same position that I had initially drifted toward
and stayed. How each dream was prolonged—vicious against peaks
or blanched smoke or any perch substantial enough to be misused.

    The soil mimicked anything gardened—was plowed, nameless. Where
men had lapped at each other—spooled wildly. Were sturdy, desirous—
a loss. Their heads misshapen only by wind. Later, by collections of sleep
and scraped bone. Some twisted heat by myself, by birds—for morning.

    A frame for this cheekless country, their dozing fell coarse.
A reckoning lacking ownership or direction, but burn anew most nights.
Those dead remained heavier. Were fitful sleep after many washes—how
nature had laid down to cuss and studded their wrists. Removed anything
smelling of pine or lilac or red.

    Others were only haggard—a vanity secured under seven months
and the first days of August. Unaware they are sick, but occupied by
fears of growing cities and their laws. How like these men, I got a job
barricading town. A locus of dead-kneed boredom or a point of heat
fanning itself outward only to cycle back and be fanned again.

    Their webby greetings were abandoned at a suspenseful pace.
Were petty-caked, brief—ignoring entire weeks or mountains.
Appearing unimportant and too deaf a reflection for anything
fully formed. But mean and sorry, we soon surrendered. Vacated the
small tearing between mate and sucker and provisioning standard.

In the same flat way that dead men are heavier. Are books of who cares. I see you that way, a dead man—my fog in barehanded heads. Again, a reenactment. Again, a rolling forgiveness. Sour, polished off—scraped onto previous reenactments. The original encounter—mourned after meals. I made like foresty light—moved on. Each man going back to angel food on a tight desk and all the sweet things bellied in muscle.

I removed myself from their look—left. Went next door to eat and bunched my food into slow webs. Remembered myself unpleasantly and spoke to another man's daughter about these memories. Spoke safely—more webs. Slept fitfully. The bed too close to the wall and no dog. The bridge of its nose wider this time—a rubric for its first ankle.

She cried, then spoke, then walked. Addressed me as a parent, addressed me carefully and slowly. Knowing how little I held. How little I spoke. Knowing my distance was short and uncaring—was only some proclamation crumpled into bulbs or a gathering to drown my smaller marriages.

)

The seeping patter of utensils—Green Street, Franklin, Elm—our configuration became filthy and single-eyed. Was a strong-held obligation to banded work. Still drooping, it refused patience or murmurs—sandy phrases which stirred slowly and hobbled. There was no letter to create any word. Remembering that when I say love, my mouth is full.

I learned then, only dully, of large transport. Of population. About neatly tucking flowers across a water's bow. About teeth puddling into lead, then being forcibly hung atop a tussock—lost rightfully in a horizon's low, but overwhelmed seat. How the town's roads were tangled into a crowded grid. Limping, not pursuing much, but met by a populated commitment. By a tracing wind.

I drank that night too—went to bed and found further seatless landscapes as I slept. I wrote back, gifting them a letter. Notes explaining my lacerated company. I neither apologized nor returned home—a tie between rail and mire and no wish to see my family.

A hair and clock traveler, I maneuvered myself further South. Stopped. Found red bedrock and games which played on soft wood and larger, but still meager coins. Like some fly in a gun—patrons worked and celebrated with eyes that were unable to move in tandem. Slapped each other's backs and fought together. A cheerful violence, scars between angry men—now less angry and happy to visit a grave.

In the east, I visited graves alone. Found the joy of being close to a stranger's bones. To and from—comforted when she called for her land and child and dog. Using the bayless names already jutted into a lake's collar—Ben, Michael, Theo. Disordered frames which ran down my shins and turned outward. Creating a second ankle—sealed within its own gesture.

Certain evenings were met with moodiness, with simple trees. A linear defeat marked by batches of yellowing daylight. A widowing strobe, like a heaved callous—easily circular or often in the formation of a rope. It burned books, then trees. Leaving small mats of leather, of metal—pressed against the last of our fruit. Recorded with the remaining ink which we couldn't replenish or understand.

Unremarkable, maybe sapless—a man was then gored and his carcass left to his wife. He was another child lost to her and she was quelled by his burial. A careful meditation chanted by a game of cards and aided by the animal that had killed him. Still too valuable to punish. Something ultimately demoted—a chalked contraption, now measured in drifts and strewn across a camp. First by perspiring, then by clinging to the dirt.

The woman's aimless story gives room for a second figure to place more wood into the burdened fire. A ceiling to cover itself—its minor papacy, formed lucklessly. How that fire had been stocked blank with tender and made slapshod. A structure that resembled clutching a mallet or clutching your hand.

Visible or nearly visible, there were more fires. Chests which expanded into crescent-shaped fibers and created strange irrigation systems—shuffled and wordy, lowlife organs protected by ribs and fat.

    At spring, junctures were given to each yarn. Were riven with slow speeds and generalist feeders. Those hackles which raise themselves along beached stems—unable to reach a smoke's height. A distance—then buried halfway between two patches of ground. Or an oval-shaped boundary containing remedies for two warring peoples. An indefinite offering—allowing exiled quarries to hold perversely broken hearts and a longing for one another. Always dispersing or exceeding. But peeled by the same germinated myth.

    This early cold snap proved to be prophetic and was honored with a common name. Each side hocked both flora and fauna—treating them as dimly, but favored witnesses to a ceremony that was rushed. A celebration winnowed from rock then woven into curtains.

    At summer, the cruelty recedes. Is burrowed away and left to settle. The soil becomes tightly bound and the townspeople claw quietly at their pale rock—cradle themselves beneath a stiffening light, then sit stagnant at their beds. Are witnesses to the sloping surface of an inherited punishment. The region's memory of debt. Pinned by the repeating roots of repeating hair and the trailing of mud.

)

Eiffel Gao

—

A Thousand Miles of My Country by Wang Xi Meng

Water sleeves flourish
double the long bridge. Thatched roof
crowns a boy in downpour.
> *Thither I came, willowy green,*
> *Hither I leave, downy snow.*

Upon this old line I woke——
snow tiptoed on my burning forehead
and the past sluiced in.
My father's reprimand rang
> *Seventeen, lucky, can't tell thick from thin…*

I turned back and saw my work:
the jumpable blue and the ensnaring green, as seen
in the eyes of poisonous beasts, glorying.

(

This forever-dawning kingdom of the East
I made home in dream and in wakefulness
would dissolve when a fisherman's Qiang flute
seined in the lament of Liangzhou
> *When all are drunk and I am alone sober*
> *When the world is muddled and I am alone clean*

Soon the snow clouds will level, the morning rays will fan out
across Her ancient scales of mountains, veins of gold
Soon the eunuchs will bustle in to collect my painting
for the Emperor in swathes of yellow brocade——

His Grand Landscape. I knew well enough
to paint only the prosperous half,
when our people in the north subsisted on a barbaric tongue,
when His Majesty laboured over a poem to commemorate
a rare rock in his fine garden as Jurchen envoys
awaited to seal an alliance He intended to break.

'He should have been born an artist, not a king.'
His most valued minister, confiscator of people's wealth,
staged me as a newly discovered protégé, and so,
the Emperor, best painter of this realm, became my master.
> *Youngster who's only donned white and grey*
> *Know thy place*

The first daylight struck the caesura of snow,
then glided on the silk scroll
along eastward meridians, northward parallels,
as my shadow coursed through
a thousand miles of China——
its brilliance illuminating for days my bare study.

My reclining country is vaster and more ruthless
than the nine-gate vermilion palace.
I have slumbered in Her bosom,
have sung to my reflection in Her opaque wine
till my friends could pour no longer,
have heard the implausible
tenderness resound along my body's gamut.

I stood in her light, once, or perhaps I mistook
its leagues of reflection flittering past me
for her gaze. Young are my bones,
but one day from them grass will spring.

This poor simulacrum of Her image
will be branded with the cinnabar imperial seal,
will change hands among the fat sleeves of powers.
But it shall live
longer than all of us at our small lives.

This is the closest I could reach
once in a lifetime.
So far out into the onrush of light,
the past subsides to an aftertaste of the chase.

Eiffel Gao

Need I return, any more?
My country laid out in between:
lush paths for her creatures
meandering to my feet.

(

In the End

    I
Your body became a winter landscape
by an old Chinese master, so faint
it can't be photographed.

    II
They clothed it in 'longevity' brocade —
the finest we could find, indigo mirror,
not for the brass of the living.

    III
This was your carriage in this world,
and we sent it to burn,
spokes and all.

    IV
The rain's purge on my hometown —
never were such rains in winter.
Your ash box sank into my arms.

    V
The weight didn't lessen whatever I promised.
Mists rose from the mountain cols
like some hermit god puffing up opium clouds.

    VI
I could never sit where you sat.
I see myself hold your vomit of blood
and drain it, over and over, down the chipped basin.

光 / 塵　Light / Dust

Fire – the upper body of 光

When the bed sheet was shaken out,
blown dust fluoresced
through pillars of light.

Perhaps we labour in a dark room,
our bodies instruments that wear and tear,
our bed a field of spice.

Man – the lower body of 光

Sometimes everything around me is revving up
to your imminent reclamation:
this lady with glowing eyes, that car glistening past,

these people spawned from a park's fibered shadows;
I feel my heart hollowing out
as they pour through.

Light and dark were one, and revered
before they were split into words.
Our species internalised fire's fluid, lurid dance

and so began our heady quest for meaning——
'One should go in fear of solitude',
Father called me back from my thoughts on his deathbed.

Water glides down polished silver. I've acquired my love's eyes.
So this is the world you see at last——
with a clarity one can't quiet.

Deer – the upper body of 麈

This was where men rounded up their prey,
where deer drummed across the plain
and their cut antlers tossed
red sequins on the yellow soil,

where dust predicted the favour of Fortune
and downy snow the pity of God.
Every palace, a cinnabar chamber,
every age, ivories and horns.

Earth – the lower body of 麈

To unpick the heavy dress of the living
to sleep in a lilac requiem

having stomached the world's onslaught   )
to rest now the will to branch out

against the dark
to renounce love

and all its omnipresent tentacles
and be freed

'I sense something is on your mind——
tell me when I wake up'

there are things love cannot save
also things death cannot bury

dust has the gentlest ways
and now you're in all the bands of light

Ode to Light

One dawn I was lifted up by a strange lightness:
my tread took no shadow, my head no feverish aim.
A bundle of light lay upon my open palms
like a harvest of sizzling gold. Years

screened past before I was tempted
to remember: tiny silver hooks of dust,
a song about an old flame, a blip in the solid sunlight
where a sparrow darted by.

(

Notes

On 'A Thousand Miles of My Country':
The painting *A Thousand Miles of My Country* has been reframed many times in the course of history. The left side of the painting seems to have been cut off, as the form of the mountain abruptly stops in the middle; with little known about the specific details of the painting's provenance, it's difficult to tell why. A totally unfounded theory is that the painter, who was said to have died within a few years of finishing this work, spirited away into the painting and, wishing to be left undisturbed, cut off the way in and the way back.

On '光 / 塵　Light / Dust':
光 means 'light' in Chinese; phrases including this character can be glory, time, brightness. 塵 means 'dust', and is related to concepts such as the world of human toil and love, and of course death. The two words, 光 and 尘, appear almost as antitheses in one Taoist doctrine and several classic Chinese poems. The character of light hasn't changed much in shape and composition, but the character of dust was simplified after the new regime of the PRC into 尘, originally 塵, the upper part resembling a deer.

)

Jacqueline Rose
–
Ink Play #1–4

(

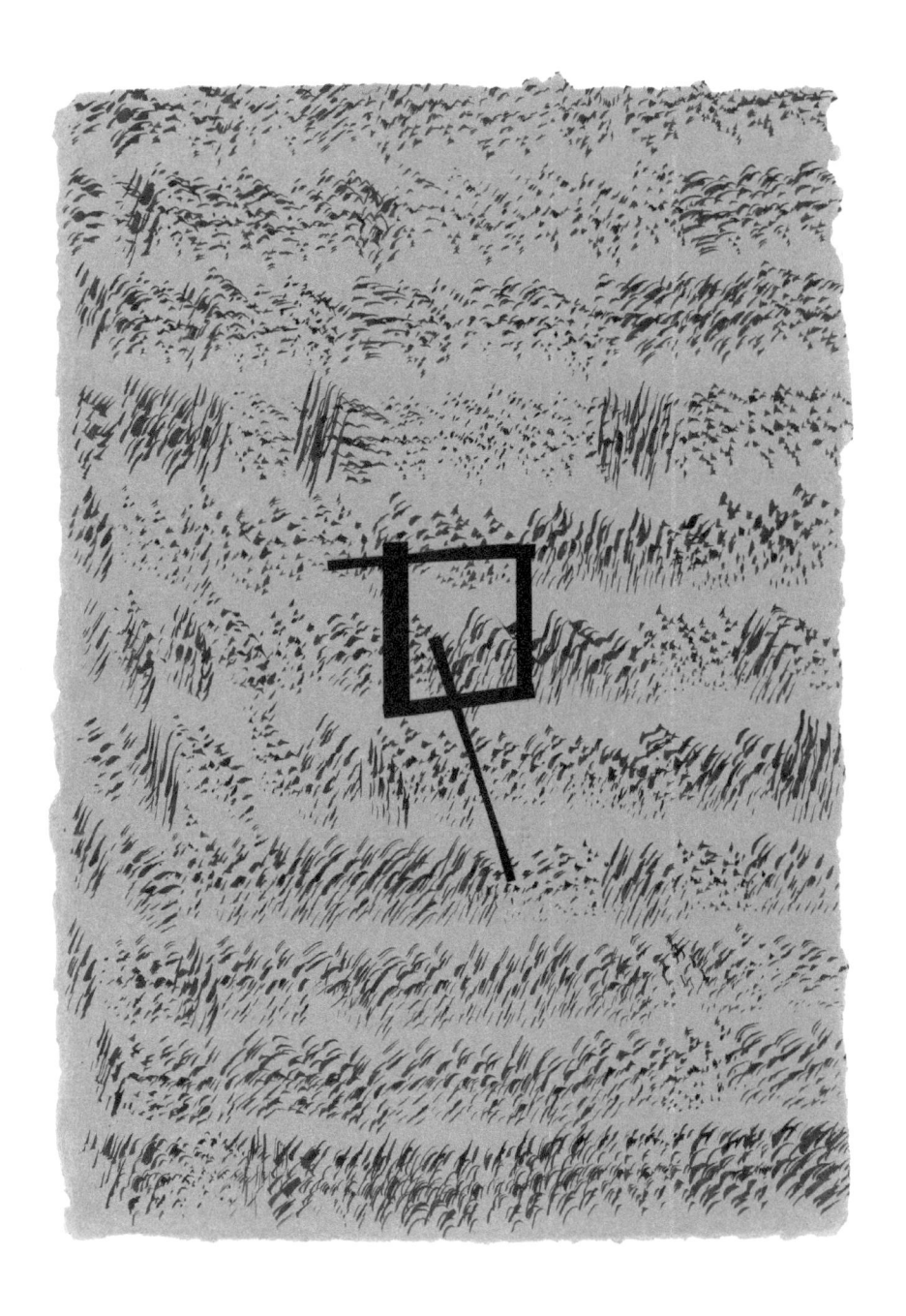

Ink Play #1   2022
Ink on paper, 42 × 30 cm

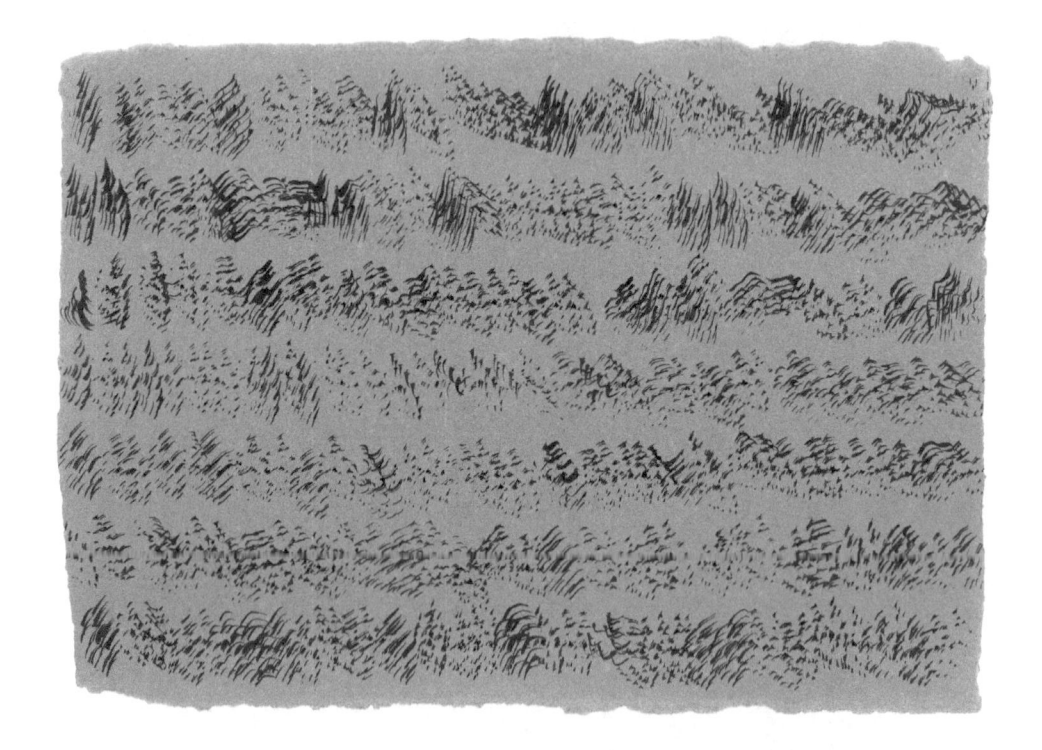

Jacqueline Rose

(

Ink Play #2 2022
Ink on paper, 31 × 43 cm

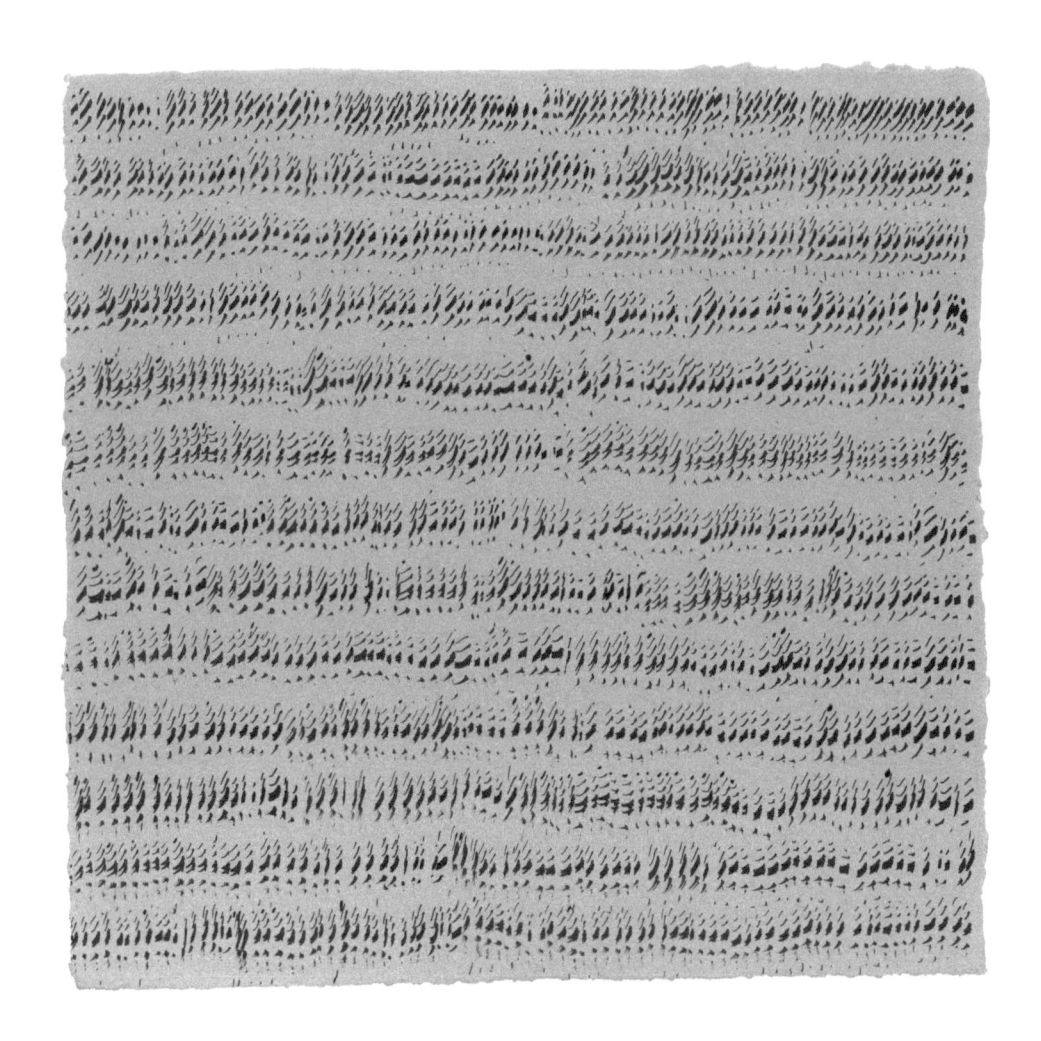

Ink Play #3   2023
Ink on paper, 50 × 52 cm

Jacqueline Rose

(

Ink Play #4   2023
Ink on paper, 30 × 30 cm

Helena Fornells Nadal

—

SAINTS

i. all the trees

a saint was there   I know how they smell   tall
he rose an arm and sunk the knife into the wound
                the wound was open already
you peeked into it and I looked at you

the space where the saint is exhibited is an art gallery
and art galleries bore me

I do not let the attendants look at me
and in order not to let them I must leave the gallery

I create a forest but the forest is wet to an extent of displeasure
I listen to the animals in it while I think of the saint   )
and you   looking at the wound and laughing loudly
so incongruous among the black uniforms of the attendants

his arm rose aided by a mechanical structure
                and fell abruptly
the wooden noise of knife against wound made us jump

in my forest birds sing more quietly
not yet turned into saints   the trees still live and stand

ii. this wet silence

                                        a loaded package from the beginning

                                                      the word *incense*
                                      relates to the act of burning

                                      a growing gap between
                                                        skin and candles

of the iron rails   the low drone   my skin or a saint's
sounds blue in dead space   the sound of doors ajar
an arm slowly bends in the liquid ebb   *pellucid* is a strange word
and flow   the automaton's grey eyes
gape underwater
                                                              I won't use it
                                      to describe the edge of a candle's flame

machinery rusts in the quarry's sleep
                                    in this memory
the jointed parts of a saintly arm   the scent of saints
raise aided by mechanical structures
and fall   the wooden noise   takes me back indoors

(of knife against wound   in the safety of the past
filled and reclaimed by silence
its wooden eyes emerge to make a temple   stations are for trains
of the blasted walls   the grooves   and churches for children
where wheels echo brim
                                      abuelo took me inside just to know awe
with wildlife   the saint   and admire the carpenter
anoints and recovers the song of birds
as my forest is remembered   hushing   I looked up towards the bodies
the lifeless face and flecks of gold
                                    saw the trees they came from
leaf flicker   the trees all gone
on the pit's floor algae   haunted by their wounds
filter the light   when family beliefs are lost
        like the holes in clouds
                                    the remains of symbols guide us
                                              in the wilderness

                                  abuelo whispered to me – the pew in the last row

                                  sat there bland and quiet

iii. grief, outdoors

in the woods their body parts
disperse and constellate
above the tallest trees
and tall, creamy, they crawl
over the blue
    upturned wild roses muscle up –
    the memorial service fails
    to fill the gaps between their heads and limbs

    ~

it was time's tiredness that hushed them
they would today agree from behind the trees
these sculptures in blue and golden silk
diffusing their voices
    I stop looking for them –
    quiet mouths say 'recede!   )
    hide in the indoor world' but
    out there, saints are still breathing
    made of wood, smooth, sweet, sunny

    ~

        their iron mechanisms survive
        but not their robes and eyes –
        charred, they've scattered
thousands of visitors will cross
the art gallery's threshold to see them –
their scriptures laughing away on wood pulp

Helena Fornells Nadal

iv. lute & vellum

it is a relief
that they are in relief
alive in contrast
with the flattened
background
you'd think their bodies are
ageing because
the gold is so heavy and
the bodies are so frail
or the wood looks so frail
they can't see it
from their angle how gold
overwhelms them
in the acts of
music & learning

(

    we can't see it
    from our angle
    how ornament
    encloses us in one
    act of loneliness
    split from the plural
    origins of branches
    but we are framed –
    the sound & light
    of those who look
    at us don't reach us
    in our ornate boxes

        only through
        the reflection of light
        from our gold
        backgrounds –
        from the edges
        of our eyes –
        do we see you

Alex Mepham

—

Live in Truth

One of us received a revelation: an open bearing. This was apparently not a sudden realisation, but a festering for months that could no longer be ignored. We were being called to live in truth, she said. And right now we were not living in truth. Herren is displeased. *How do we live in truth?* we asked. She could not answer, only stared into us with her throat constricting and tears streaming down her cheeks. On occasion her lips would shape the words: *live in truth.* We began to change our ways. First we forwent meat, then fish, then any foodstuff entwined with breath. But her weeping did not stop. We no longer adorned the table with flowers from the valley but with bowls of liquid from the marsh. Though these bowls we gave up collecting when her weeping did not cease. But as her tears dried up her face set to flint towards us. *It is time to live in truth,* she announced, and we followed her through the grasses. We knew the change was imminent, and we did our best to prepare. Still, the smallest of us were unable to change. And, yes, they suffered the most. They could not live in truth.

Apostate Encounters the Rat Virgin
after Henrik Ibsen's Lille Eyolf

and i am led out one night / past the houses / the storefronts / to the water / i heard her mouth-harp / she called my name / i am taken to the strand / where she stands / clothed in cement / and the thousand eyes of her children / the ones called to the water / she speaks to me / asks me what worries me / what is kribbling / krabbling inside of me / she wants to take care of me / to comfort me / to release me of my sour apple / she casts her charm / creeps / glacial and creaking / towards the water / no need for her boat / she takes me with her / drawing me in / dyp / dyp / to my long sweet sleep / to where it is quiet / cosy / and dark / where there is no gnawing / no biting / she has called my name / called me / *velsignet* / as i sink / dyp / among her farewells / among her thousand farewells

(

Apostate Addressed by the Voices
    after Henrik Ibsen's Rosmersholm

A-pos-ta-sy!   it mumbled
A-pos-ta-sy!   this murmur

I tried to still: the rustling
between the cabins   the panels

of the stave church   soon
these whispers collapsed

into a croaking   from every brook
and stream and river   rushing

from the forests: *A-pos-ta-sy!*
A-pos-ta-sy!   I saw the sky

darken   murked with snow
falling thick on frozen lakes

and hardened earth   against
window panes that masked

the blizzard   howling: *A-pos-ta-sy!*
A-pos-ta-sy!   until that snarl-

sharp night   what I'd been
expecting arrived: the white horse

he eased up the mill-path
to my door   his burr

beckoned me out: come
he said   let me take you away

let's withdraw from here
dear companion   dear apostate

let's withdraw   from this false
and ambiguous position

Stephen Watts

—

Men Drinking Together

Men drinking together
murmuring hardly talking
or haggling & getting-by

Getting by in the loneliness
of their eyeshot shut-eye !

In the redness of their ears,
in the fain drunkenness of pig-
hostels, the attitude of berets
& bonnets, tired generosities
carried through born bodies

Men drinking together
getting by, supporting each other,
calm in the aftermath of work

In the depths of their snows
& in their cavernous silences

Just there where a string-
bridge crosses their void –

Dark angel bring us to water !

Men drinking together
palming loneliness on lager
getting by with beer bellies
with palm-wine, with bolts
or batches of toddy

Men drinking together, men
unable to tell their pain.

Half An Hour In The Thomas Neale

That someone I love might walk through the door

That the old man from Galway might get to recover
                the traces of his childhood

That the wild children playing pool out back might
            grow to know beauty in terror

Or no-one in these generations ever will share these
                archived generosities

That the zip on Seamas's jacket should open to music,
            all of it grace notes and danger

That the old woman walking past with her shopping
            who never comes in, should one time   )
                      come

That those come up from the shire of the pigs should
            retain open hearts in the pomp of their
                    warring

That the painting of the wall should come alive and
            all of us dance in the calms of our fury

That we might all share together the gift of the gab,
                the graft of the gob

That I might be able to read these garbled scripts
        when I get home from this pub

That someone I love might walk through the door ...

Leonie Rushforth
—
Moon Setting

'...nothing to be sad about'

for Frances

The plane tree's winter nets have snagged
a consolation magpie but the moon

gives them the slip, imperturbable and positively
sailing down into the north west

swelling as she goes. Look how she glows
and softens, her halo turning milky. The sky

(

is hers and we her gaping subjects — when

all at once she drops behind the houses
as into a slot.
                    She's let fall, this.

It's for you, I mean it's that which is yours — legally,
tenderly in this economy of daughters.

Floods

There was a point last night when the rain
became a storm. The wind got up
and rushed through the gardens. I could hear
the trees thrashing and hissing. Something empty
rattled around a small space for hours.

The morning blue of the sky was so blue it was daunting.
Nothing seemed equal to its proposal.
I thought of my mother alone with her body, how
she can't say the word *death*.

The forecast is a screenful of triangles warning of floods.
It takes twenty-four hours for the waters to rise,
before the rivers erase.

)

A Drowning

Last night my mother drowned.
When I think – I can't be sure – but I think I saw her go
or arrived at the quay just after to see something
pale and loosening loosened from its shape
fall away under a moored hull,
clothes twisting slowly around the limbs
and lifting pale & green – at all events I knew
whether I saw or not I knew
she was in the water and slowly falling and found
I'd followed fully clothed, felt the coat I had on
double its weight and drag at my purpose.
The surrounding world was telling me she'd gone.
Did I hesitate? I did. Then a decision
took hold, the water turned dark and there was
nothing to see. It was I'm now thinking her will
at last to go, how it took on its form in water
and was fulfilled, its winding sheet
my most devout & most daughterly wish.

Oisín Roberts

—

Double Life

-It ain't perfect nothing is-
-There's still room to grow-
-Feeling different staying in-
-Made a little home-
-So when I sit back in my chair-
-As the evening wanes-
-I don't remember getting here-
-But I'm glad I came-

My friend Emma told me about a Beckett play about someone's last tape. It was about a man who recorded a tape every day recounting the day. He's at the end of his life, rewinding back to random points and the audience gets the story in that way. And I was thinking that's how I am, all the time. That patchy place is how I remember things/my life and how I read when I'm not concentrating and how I write most of the time. Crap. Crap's Last Tape.

I just turned 30 in March. I hadn't ever thought about age that much until I was turning 30 and everyone around me was shocked and telling me how big of a deal it was all the time. I caught that bug or a bug like it and became really reflective over the few months before my birthday.

I've been thinking about home a lot. I don't think it's a birthday thing. As in, I don't think it's really a Pisces thing. I don't even think it's a homesick thing. Big parts of me think it's about the ongoing genocide happening in Palestine. When I think of Gaza, Palestine, as I do in all my moments, every day, it makes me think about home. And it makes me want to talk about home, in all the different ways. I'm from Derry (when this piece was just notes, I read them out – to an English audience, in a venue in London – so I had '(explain?)' written down beside that). Derry has a historic solidarity with Palestine. I learned that 'our struggle' and 'their struggle' could dissolve and should dissolve in solidarity. Free Derry, Free Palestine. Recently my mam sent me an enamel pin badge of the Irish flag and the Palestinian flag together. The second time that I read the notes out, someone in the audience who was also from Ireland gave me a badge of Free Derry corner, in the colours and shapes of the Palestinian flag.

I'm not sure I liked the small city where I grew up. (Pure shock there from everyone gay.) Looking back, I struggled with it, but more than that, I didn't think about it that much. It felt like it took me a really long time to imagine leaving. I moved a lot from house to house, then from area to area. It became more common for people to go to England for university. Some people started to move to Australia for jobs and money. I feel it might be embarrassing to admit, or it feels complicated to reflect on my youthful naivety here – but in my thinking about home a lot and this not-thinking-about-my-home much, I'm connecting how that was really a privilege, right? That this non-feeling isn't something my great granny got to feel. Or my granny. Or probably not my ma either. Because their home was under threat of being taken away from themby the Brits until it wasn't anymore, and then mines wasn't. (This is the idea of generational trauma that I learned about at university.)

I think about 'home' over morning coffee when I listen to Palestinians tell their story. Their story of coming home to their house as rubble and their siblings are underneath. I'm crying for them and their home. I march and rally for them because everything is being taken. And somehow more than everything has been taken since the time of writing.

I think we should work hard to connect. I'm thinking about, relating to this, a way that I have always made these connections is by really listening. That might come from my upbringing or culture or both. Have you ever heard a group of Irish people talking to each other? All talking – in statements and questions and replies – at once. You're half way through asking me something and I am already replying because I know where you are going, and I'm going there with you. It's not because I feel I know better than you or even that I just want to interrupt. But I understand you.

I wanted to say, if you know how I grew up, which you don't. But if you did. There is another way of really, active listening that comes from that. To listen as a means of always needing to know what is going on, where everyone is and how they are feeling. I'm a big music head. That's from my upbringing. Everyone on my mam's side is. My uncle, my mam's brother, was a guitar tech for bands when I was younger. When they would play the local music venue he could swing a special access pass that meant I could see the gig even though I was underage and didn't pay for a ticket. Maybe this didn't happen a lot, but I remember that it did. It was cool to have that sticker and it was cool to put it on your thigh like the boys who were in bands and techs for the bands did. I saw a lot of cool bands that way – like Biffy Clyro – maybe that's not cool now but it was. I still go to gigs a lot, I still aim for the barrier, I still mosh, I'm still curious about guitarists' pedal boards, I still listen out for the guitar tuning before songs and name the one coming if I can hear it, to myself, in my head, I mostly go alone or out loud, to whoever has come with me – it doesn't matter to me.

In Ireland there is this weird thing called 'disco dancing', I haven't come across it here but imagine young girls wearing a lot of fake tan and make-up, with hair done up in big, straight, spikey ponytails. Sometimes they wear dresses, sometimes they wear bodysuits or leggings and everything is colourful and very sparkly. I think they look strange? Imagine you're in a big school hall and you're all – the audience – pinned to the edges. The music is some genre of electronic, rave music with simple beats and very high-pitched, auto-tuned singing. Like a baby. Then the disco dancers run. Full speed and in circles. They kick their legs up really high and they often put one arm up in the air at the same time, slightly behind them and spread their fingers very wide apart. You're just watching.

I like my brother so much but we haven't ever had the type of relationship where I felt I could ask him for anything. After seeing some disco dancing at school I wanted the song they danced to on my mp3 player. dj cammy – dancing in the dark. It wasn't cool to want this. My brother invited me into his room, or were we in my room? He was teaching me how to download music, telling me about LimeWire. I remember trying to get the information off him then getting him to go, so I could download the uncool music by myself but he wanted to show-by-doing. A way of learning that I actually went on to really respond to well. I reluctantly told him the song was called dancing in the dark. *wot by springsteen?* I didn't understand who that was, but I did understand that he was so impressed in a way, so I just said *aye*. At some point I did listen to the Springsteen song and loved it. I even eventually used my new knowledge of LimeWire to download Springsteen's entire back catalogue and get really into 'Highway Patrolman' at a young age. That's about brothers, actually.

I don't know if he knows but I got a lot of my music through him and I got it through this really, active listening I'm on about. In the house I'm picturing (we shared lots of houses over the years) his bedroom was around the corner and down the landing from mine. I would hear him playing something on the computer – or I think he might have been the first person I heard playing music through his phone while he showered – and I'd type the lyrics into our shared, family computer.

I found so much that way. Some stuff that kinda fell away, like Modest Mouse or Death Cab for Cutie. But then also some stuff that really stuck and I still listen to most days, like Elliott Smith and Bright Eyes.

-It ain't simple like before-
-These are different times-
-No longer worried about getting bored-
-Just trying to clear my mind-
-From all the noise out there-
-All the spooks all the moving parts-
-Cameras everywhere I look imitating art-

Mica Georgis

—

from *Oh...Mallards!!*

Oh ... Mallards!!

**An excerpt from a film
by Mica Georgis**

)

1   EXT. IDYLLIC LAKE IN THE ENGLISH COUNTRYSIDE – DAWN

A WIDE STATIC SHOT:

FIVE 'MALE' MALLARD DUCKS resting atop a lake, poised in a perfectly straight line. The DUCKS face eastwards ready for their cue – in the centre of the frame, in the centre of the lake. Spring is in the air – wild flowers and grass burst along the banks. Dawn is breaking – sumptuous pinks and purples fill the sky. The DUCKS' iridescent green heads and bright yellow beaks catch the soft morning light. A romantic scene – the rural idyll. The image is painterly in its composition, colour and texture. The frame breathes gently – the water ripples, the ducks wag their tails – everything is alive.

An original soundtrack underscores, ethereal and otherworldly, building gradually as the scene progresses. Sounds of the water and ducks bubble through the soundtrack. In the background, parallel to the ducks, a blanket of artificial mist makes its way from the left-hand side of the frame across the lake. As it hits the right edge of the frame the CAMERA and DUCKS start to move in unison –

The journey begins!

Offscreen the troupe is directed by a visionary CHOREOGRAPHER. They are incisive and intuitive, deeply in tune with their dancers.

They give notes throughout the rehearsal. It is close to opening night.

    Choreographer: & 1,2,3 & breath

A ONE-TAKE SMOOTH CONTINUOUS PARALLEL TRACKING SHOT:

The RAFT OF MALLARDS slowly make their way to dry land. One by one they jump up onto the bankside & continue in formation across the grass.

    Choreographer: Chin up, soft landing

As the third duck lands –

    Choreographer: Perfect landing, &...

They have rehearsed this routine before. As the THIRD DUCK exits the lake, the camera pulls back and slows down on the FOURTH & FIFTH DUCK, cutting the first three out of frame. The CAMERA then moves forward to reveal the THIRD DUCK who has transformed into YASSER, a handsome trans man in his 30s, concealed inside of a mallard duck furry suit.

    Choreographer: (a sharp intake of breath, in awe)

We have borne witness to a spectacular transformation. He is visually striking – tight feathers, glassy eyes, a long shiny beak. A realistic match. He moves both as duck and human. He is comfortable in his creatureliness.

    Choreographer: & Yasser, arms back

YASSER slots precisely into the line. THE BROOD continue on their journey as though nothing is out of the ordinary. YASSER reaches his arms back, widening his chest.

They make their way to a wide open field with a large outdoor festival stage in the centre. The limits of the stage are visible, a metal truss structure with stage lights rigged to the frame, facing out towards the audience.

    Choreographer: A force is pulling you
    towards the stage...

    Choreographer: You are drawn to something

As if by magic, directly in THE BROOD'S line of sight is a staircase that leads up to the main stage. One by one they climb up the stairs.

Choreographer: 1,2,3,4 1,2,3,4

The FOUR MALLARD DUCKS & YASSER line up across the full length of the stage, evenly spaced out. Simultaneously the CAMERA tracks back to take in the whole stage & its surroundings.

Choreographer: Nice tight positions

In one movement, the FIFTH DUCK takes its position and the CAMERA comes to rest. We land on a STATIC SHOT in line with the centre of the stage. A perfectly symmetrical frame. In sync, to the beat of the music, with the precision of a troop of tightly choreographed dancers, they all turn clockwise to face the audience. The morning sun breaks through behind them, backlighting the stage.

Choreographer: Lights up

The routine begins... One by one the lights around the stage come on, starting from the bottom left of the stage climbing clockwise around to the top and back down to the bottom right.

(Da—DA da—DA da—DA)

The stage awakens!

BEAT

Choreographer: gather all your energy
in your core...

can I see the feathers come up...
before you...

(breath)...take-off

The DUCKS all take off in sync, flying high above the stage & up into the sky, out of frame. YASSER is left standing in the middle of the stage – his large glassy eyes staring directly into the camera. The focus is all on him. He was born to be a star!

>Choreographer: and ac-tion!

A spectacular display of fireworks flies above the stage, filling the sky with sparkling Disney-esque illuminations. Overlaid on top of the real fireworks appears the title 'OH...MALLARDS!!' in illustrious VFX fireworks. The music reaches a crescendo!!! As the fireworks fade out YASSER lifts his arms back and bends his legs as he prepares to take off –

The shot stills momentarily, like a photograph. If you look closely you can see the image breathing gently behind YASSER, the trees swaying in the wind.

The image comes alive again – the CHOREOGRAPHER walks up the stairs from stage left into frame, YASSER relaxes his body.

>Choreographer: Great work, let's take
>10, cool off
>>(they look up to the sky)
>all of you

)

CUT.

2   EXT. IDYLLIC LAKE – A WARM SPRING DAY

YASSER, in human-size mallard form, is paddling across the lake, enjoying his morning swim. He creates a V-shaped ripple of waves behind him. He is travelling across the lake from the direction of the main stage (from the right- to left-hand side of the frame). Everything is calm – the soundtrack has the feel of relaxing spa music playing inside of a video game, including the sounds of artificial water and bubbles. He is closely followed by the CAMERA, which acts as another MALLARD sitting atop the lake, journeying alongside him.

The sunlight catches the side of his face, he is wildly attractive & he knows it. As the MALLARD/CAMERA's gaze lingers on him, a FLOCK OF THREE MALLARDS enter the frame, soaring through the sky above them, the length of their wing-span in full view.

They are also travelling from the direction of the main stage, at a slight downwards slope. They look majestic and serene as they slow down, flying against the wind, towards the water. The MALLARDS all land on the water, at slightly different times, as one. As they hit the water they create explosive splashes, leaving a trail behind them that quickly dissipates. They join YASSER, moving as one body, gliding through the water.

The sunlight hits the water, creating a natural spotlight on one of the MALLARDS. The water glistens around them, dancing and sparkling, encircling them with sun glitter. They continue to move through the water together, the sunlight following them. The MALLARD/CAMERA & FLOCK move leisurely, in synchronicity, going about their day. The CAMERA then overtakes the flock towards the bankside. The camerawork feels like a smoothly choreographed dance.

A DRONE SHOT:

The MALLARD/CAMERA exits the water, hovering above the ground at the eye level of a MALLARD. It lands smoothly on the bankside, in the middle of a pathway lined by lush wild grass. The path curves, obscuring the end point. The CAMERA moves smoothly down the pathway, drawn towards something unidentifiable at the other end.

At some point along the journey a MALLARD smoothly intercepts the camera from behind, as if appearing from inside the camera. It takes the lead, its hips moving from side to side. The CAMERA follows from behind, transfixed on the MALLARD, transfixed on an unknown destination. In one smooth movement the CAMERA overtakes the MALLARD & then YASSER overtakes the camera from behind. It is as though we are inside a video game, opening up into new portals. YASSER then leads the CAMERA on the final stretch of the journey. The CAMERA slows down, pausing, taking in his full body. The pathway leads to an opening. In the centre of the alcove, atop a circular rotating stage, stands AISHA, a trans popstar. They are in their 30s, with glowing skin, no make-up. The stage glows like a lightbox underneath them.

Both the CAMERA & YASSER are drawn to this place, pulled by a force outside of their control. The CAMERA fixes in position, at enough of a distance to take in the stage, and AISHA'S full body.

MID STATIC SHOT:

AISHA is dancing on a podium, a slow sultry routine usually performed inside a private room at a strip club. Their body is glistening, oily and covered in tattoos, with a tightly-shaven head, in a shiny triangle bikini, a white tank top and platform crocs. They emanate an effortless sexiness. They rub their hands down their chest & against their tits, down their waist & across their ass. They slowly pull their tank top off, their body rolls through the air. They lean in and tease the camera closer. They are incredibly seductive. It is at once a performance for themselves, for YASSER and for the CAMERA. YASSER is aroused, pearls of sweat line the back of his neck, hidden underneath his suit. AISHA reaches out their hand out & invites YASSER onto the stage.

    Aisha: Come here baby

    Yasser: If you insist

AISHA observes YASSER with a glint in their eye, YASSER takes in AISHA, in awe.

    Yasser: Why me?

AISHA smiles coyly. YASSER moves towards AISHA, AISHA stops him.

    Aisha: I saw you rehearsing...

Fame has brought him more than he could ever imagine.

    Aisha: No hands

    Yasser: Whatever you say

YASSER is salivating. AISHA could stop the proceedings at any moment, they hold all of the control. AISHA starts rubbing up against YASSER, dry humping his wet skin.

    Yasser: I've not got long

AISHA seductively puts their finger to his lips. They are both incredibly horny – AISHA could be playing, YASSER is serious. The tension builds. They are on the verge of a joint orgasm. A cacophony of quacks explodes from YASSER. All the Ducks join in utter ecstasy. A breathy chorus –

(Quackquackquackquackquack!!!!

CUT.

Galia Admoni

—

On Sunday 30th April at the Tate Modern, Wendy and I look at sculptures, paintings, art films and photographs, and Wendy obsesses over the content guidance sign outside

A retelling of the day is a form of collage:

                    of things salvaged
                    of things charred
            of things reconstructed and simplified
of objects emphasising an interconnectedness with forces larger than ourselves
of objects evoking the subversive power of artists' previous work
of pieces unifying disparate elements like fragments of furniture alongside florals, to create a new kind of harmony
of pieces reflecting disruptions between creation and destruction
of delicate paintwork pierced with violence, with holes that are deeply inviting – galvanic, like the potential for orgasm
of Wendy saying that the paintings we see are my poems in art forms
of the sign that declares that *This display shows photography and film where artists use their bodies in performances as a form of activism*
of the fact that this is a perfect rendering of Wendy's poems

)

Further evidence that you are a true agent of chaos

Once when I was eight I invited ten friends to see the view from the top of a building for my birthday party. Only seven came but that was ok, seven was enough for a celebration. When they all arrived though, it was clear they didn't actually want to be there. As we started to climb, each step was a ringing out of *Why didn't she want to go dry ski slope skiing?* or *I can't believe my mum made me come to this!* but I didn't care. I wanted to scale this building. I had to. There was something about the way it rose above it all that appealed to me. Was it aspirational? I didn't know much back then, but I somehow knew I would feel better when I was at the top. It turned out to be a cloudy day though, even in June, and the only way any of us could see the view from our short eight-year-old bodies was by taking turns to stand on each other's shoulders, peering through convenient breaks in the cloud bank when they presented themselves. This wasn't a great strategy because we were eight, and weak, and also no one really cared about the view except me. A few of my friends took pity on me after a while and tried to lift me up. Once or twice I was able to see a snapshot of green below. It looked velvet. I wanted more. We tried again and I saw tiny toy cars circling as if on tracks, like they had no choice. One last try allowed for an image of a haybale on fire. This, it turned out, was the last straw.

I fell from my friend's shoulders, directly on to my hands and knees, and I cried. There was blood. I blinked through the tears and then it turned out it wasn't my eighth birthday after all, it was yesterday, and the building was your functional marriage to someone else and your published books, and the friends were all my failed relationships and unfinished poems and high-functioning anxiety, and the cloud bank was the thing that meant we stopped talking properly, and the tears were, well they were actually, to be fair, just tears.

)

Confetti as instruction

Jack says *did you give her the full minute on the chain?* and I've obviously missed a whole saga. Unravelled streamers speak of feverish revelry but how long can we keep these empty bottles on the counter? How many days after can we pretend a night can be remade? Leave the bin bags in the cupboard? Return to a scene to rethink it? Return to a night repeatedly but never get to the truth of it? A party where there was never a plan.

It's like that with me most of the time. I am someone you can never get to the end of.

And in some ways, it's actually fine. And in some ways, it's a total hell.

Eloise Bennett

—

🌿✷ **sky-watching with RA Walden's *access points***

In recent weeks I've noticed marks in fields and wastelands: bent nodes, sections flattened by bodies passing through or resting, vehicles turning, or wind through the crops. I think back on the live-feed congressional sessions featuring non-human biologics, reverse engineering vehicular debris, conspiracy, doubt and denial. Watching from train windows, down overgrown lanes and on walks at the edge of town, I wonder what these markings and movements might portend.

When I visited RA Walden's studio last year a large drawing on paper was taped to the white wall. The paper hosts six related ink drawings depicting molecular structures; each is made up of round circles, filled in with black ink, connected by concentric lines. They do not fill the page but gather together in the top half of the sheet. The markings show the structure of the six most common elements on Earth: carbon, hydrogen, nitrogen, oxygen, phosphorus and sulphur. Rovers and space probes are programmed to seek out these molecules on other planets, caching samples and producing reports. In searching for these, the vehicles and probes scan for evidence of ancient life or future habitable environs.

Each of Walden's drawings might be a map or score, composed of moments for movement and rest. Several months later, they exist as large-scale, perforated aluminium structures evoking crop circles on a sloping bank in upstate New York. Hovering just above the surface of the Earth, light shifts and reflects across them, and they are transfigured, too, by accompanying writings, sonic works and a research archive.

Walden's work brings together fragments of thinking and feeling across crip time, illegible states of the body and the entwined lives of these molecules. Their writings draw attention to the constant co-constitution of bodies and environments, re-grounding sickness as part of this, in soil, cloud, ash, a spiralling snail shell, the glow of sulphur burning.

Sound pieces by Walden and artist-composer The Honorable Elizabeth A. Baker weave through unfamiliar terrains. I hear: breath, lamenting, metallic heaving, drones and birdsong, a whispered word caught in my throat. Sounds dissolve and echo, defying stillness and resonating between the six compositions. Evoking molecular intimacy, these works bring our landed bodies into direct connection with bodies of land, emphasising the vulnerabilities of both.

An aerial photograph captures a flattened image of the sculpture, shot from a drone; this one maps the structure of oxygen in sheets of welded aluminium. A glimpse of silver in a green square. The structure rests on the grass, and different foliage is visible beneath and beside it. A subtitle text at the bottom of the image reads: *every body is an echo of something that happened*.

In metal, words and sound, Walden conceives of sickness as a form of visitation: the arrival and presence of an (uninvited) other, dwelling with and hosting. Visitation can refer to the appearance of a celestial or supernatural being – sometimes sacred, sometimes unwelcome. It can manifest as both divine punishment and blessèd encounter.

Knowledge about extra-planetary visitation and crop circles has been treated with disdain and disbelief, categorised as falsehood. These supposed hoaxes range through inexplicable visions, airship sightings, deathbed revisions, crash site surveys and carefully itemised debris. The visitation of sickness is one which similarly incites a demand for proof, validity and legitimacy. Walden's work asks us to listen closely to the echo of disdain towards crop circles, as they appear in the field and by the roadside, connecting it to the disbelief directed towards the experiences and needs of disabled people.*access points // or // alternative states of matter(ing)* circles the aftermath of visitation: the drawn-out moment of change in which what was familiar becomes unrecognisable.

access points considers how we might be changed by the visitation of sickness, and more broadly by our ceaseless and reciprocal impact on one another as earthly bodies, bodies of earth. Walden's work recalls to us this contingency and forges connections with extra-terrestrial forms of life. Their work mirrors this lack of fixity, the constant reconfiguration of visitation and change.

A composite image combines three screenshots from a website; the site presents research on UFOs and crop circles, as published in magazines, books and journals from the 1980s and 1990s. The screenshots include images of *The Crop Watcher* magazine, trail-cam footage, mysterious lights in the sky, bent and flattened shapes in fields of crops, and short texts comprising 'sighting diaries'.

With RA at their studio, I looked through a collection of publications arranged in small piles on the floor. This ephemera documents decades of attentive sky-watching and field observation, a developing lexicon, and instances of participation through the reporting of circles and sightings. Scans of these appear in Walden's website for the project, a meticulous catalogue of captured images, video footage, samples and diagrams. The reports remind me of my own writings to record recurring pain, as though an archive of phone notes might constitute accepted evidence. Walden's work acts to archive these publications, with their visions of interconnected organisms, receptive states, mysterious happenings and transfiguration. Self-published, carefully folded and stapled, they assemble a lore around extraterrestrial visitation, the body and the land.

The notion of *hoax* through which crop circles are dismissed has links to phrases of faux-Latin, magic and sonic hauntings. Hoaxing is usually negatively imbued, related to forms of deceit and conspiracy. But in Walden's work, the hoaxed offers a place to glimpse the unseen, to deviate from accepted forms of knowledge and to assemble a research methodology that dwells in unknowing. To conspire is, here, to weave narrative, symbol and language around phenomena and experiences that are deemed inexplicable, intangible and/or non-existent. Through sculpture, poetry, audio and video Walden maps our elemental connections, parallels our bodily and planetary vulnerabilities, sickness and visitation, while reflecting on change, transformation, doubt and new methods for survival. I wonder about how we might conspire as communities through these poetic modes: like the sky-watchers comparing notes, commoning evidence, building in contestation and reconciliation.

(

—

Walden's work operates as a point of ingress that connects and leads me to others. If there's a sound behind my thinking here it is Mica Levi's tracks for *Under The Skin*, and their collection of scores *STAR STAR STAR*.

I checked the Nasa Voyager mission status website after a friend coincidentally updated me on the whereabouts of Voyager 1: it has been in interstellar space for over a decade now but will remain within our solar system for another 14,000 years, minimum. I listened to Laurie Spiegel's realisation of Johannes Kepler's *Harmonices Mundi* which features on the Voyager Golden Record, a phonograph disc aboard the probe, intended to be listened to by extraterrestrial life.

Walden's poems recall to me CAConrad's guidance for creating (Soma)tic Poetry Rituals, as well as wider concrete poetry experiments, as modes of writing that frequently enact a lytic breakdown of the space between sound, words and page.

access points // or // alternative states of matter(ing) was on view at Storm King Art Centre from 20 May to 13 November 2023. Documentation of the project, including the sound pieces and poems, are hosted on Storm King's website and at: accesspointsrawalden.com

James Rodker

—

**RELIQUARY TRANSLATIONS,
GLIMPSES (18 - 20 - 29 - 32)**

)

James Rodker

The matanza   the burying of the pig   still ringing
in my mind as I walked with no camera through the leaning streets of Burgos
grids without edges and archways overhead   tearing papery husks
from the wasp nest   *bodies that listen like faces,*
and lift themselves like arms;   *chains of bodies, garlands and single*
organisms;   *bodies that listen like faces and lift tendrils*
and heavy clusters of bodies into which sin's sweetness rises out of the roots
of pain   the grid can only ever   be repeated.
and in the darkroom I watched as the Arco de Santa María came forth like rain
and in the cloisters *I am what I became.*   (one should never be love in Burgos)
snowfall as if you were still merely sleeping   nice to hold when I'm tired
at St. Bernard's Well by the Water of Leith she told me how long it had taken
and in the background arrondissements of 19th and 12th (the rugs were hung
on the walls)   *becoming cyclonic*   and soaked
in condensing fumes   of voiced   exaltation   and settling
ribbons of grief   (echoes   as simple   as stains
that lingered   like dying   belief)
we are Just (now)   *remembering*   *how long sounds can last*
and only (just) *now become civilized*   (*we want to hear sounds continuous*)
and in the background tapestries of heaven, on the back of the ferry at dawn,
and in ligaments torn while dancing, and there, In a Moment Divine

(

and in the sun I saw you there waiting, on the steps of Saint-Philippe-du-Roule
in blazing hail by the boatshed (promising to return to Bristol) to build a home
that leaked beneath the windows when it rained, and in dry sunlight smelled
of tobacco and balsamic vinegar,   and to know we were happiest together
and to never   (of each other)   go hungry.
when I had still to meet you,   and dangled in sunlight off the Mánes Bridge
(in thick particulate air)   in flames lifted his head and running / in sunlight
macerated pear   ((((sung in castrato)   down marble steps)
hung half a carcass)   washed my hands)   (and wept
(backed by white tiles   with a glass   of cold patxaran))
My Lights Kiss Your Thoughts Every Moment   there is no one
after the other   (when all the sparrows left the roof   at once)
in to and out of the mustard fields   *you're somewhere else*   he told me
you go somewhere else completely   (was whispered quickly   in my ear)
if a slice of orange in summer wine   is all we have to eat
on the dusty midnight streets   of Burgos
as awnings of cafés and pharmacies flocked   in hot sirocco wind
Burgos,   and Porto,   Lausanne,   and Bordeaux
Eli,   *Eli,*   *Eli,*   where the islands go

in grey Piraeus   and on the ferry   just leaving
you showed me the scratch   in your eye

    willing to die   for ideas
(thoughtless ideas)
        at the Sparagmos

in winds sweet with smoke and pine resin
behind blonde images
        you didn't wake me when you left

and later   in the market   found Blake in Greek and Simplified
Chinese   *Falling Water Lullaby*
Adoration of the Name
        that dream   again
where I circle   the old   city wall

upon waking   and hearing   the death of Brian McBride
and *Overture* and cried   for other losses
    Dopamine Clouds   *Over Craven Cottage*
shoulders   under   the waves   )

spinal   column   fluid   suspended   in oil
    harvested their blue dyes   from sea snails   (*Blue, purple,*
and scarlet thread,   *and linen,*   *and goat hair,*   *And ram skins*
dyed red,   *and tachash skins,*   *and acacia wood,*
    Oil for the light,   *spices*   *for anointing*)

an ache   that could not be placed   but for the Rue Gabrielle
on orange hotel carpet   listening to the air   conditioning
    August and new September   over   the phone

if it was not for Picton Street
        Stapleton, Church, or Gloucester
if it was not   for feet cut down   to the bone
twelve men drowned   laid out on the parish church tables
ripe with ink and wrapped in the flags of the sea

stepped out   of a wood   panelled room   into sunlight
        (if it was not   for the tree)

James Rodker

    we either died, or were born, beneath argan trees
    necks and legs and teeth of goats like butter
    surfaced and peeling the burnt away skin
    (threw his rosehip tea on the fire)

    and after his January
    suicide by cocaine
    on 6th Avenue

                            went about like a man in a trance

    and on to Madame Marie's
    in the snow (to get warm
    in the dance)

                      the chapel on the ward
(had no windows,

                    in a red chalk copse
                    of birch

    Buddha (Field) streaming
    tears of sparkling
    water

                Tyskies on the way to the viewpoint over the gorge
                the frosted glass window the sun was still warm
                half five and the sun was still setting
                told me *lasting was love*

    told me *anything I do from now*
    would be seen from above

someone   practising   saxophone
         and the window   open
to the August   evening   air

someone with their temple   to the purple   window
         of the evening   train   and the bonfire
still   in their hair

Instant Loveland   over solar panels
                                          and the window over the wing
scars under shaved head
                                  heard butterflies

Instant Loveland   at the end of vespers   in the doorway
to the Place Chapelet
                                  stiff hands   in the cold

         as it had come   *out of the veins;*   *the changing*
                     of colour
                                                       (Patutsky   *)*
         in Paradise)
                                  with grainy footage   of the loving dead

when I had still to meet you   and stood waiting on the banks of the Douro
         in shifting vapours   of pomegranate   wax

and nitrous oxide summers climbing trees in the dark   behind the bus depot
         running home   with yellow/green   bruises

chewing on the feeling of trying to tell you   for the first time
         in the shadow   of the Tour de la Chaîne

         and by the second time it was November   and it was meant
                  as strong as I'd felt it   and was said quickly
                                  in the corner   of the room

Duncan Montgomery
—
Ever is the eye

      'my dear sisters, love your windows as little as possible.'
      — *The Ancrene Wisse*

The chick is fixed, fixated; it is stuck
to the lip of the nest. It drips its hunger
into the stirred suspension of air stippled
    with insects:

midges, mayflies, every speck of lusty summer
itching to distract me, I've been sat here
almost twenty minutes, drawn to what I
    can't quite see:

(a hemisphere of shadow, moss and down:
of pipped and cracked and shat-about eggshells,
trash that youth entails. The chick is blameless
    if it fails.

A/P   Montgomery

Duncan Montgomery

Sir Gawain & the Green Knight

on foot
on field
in town
by night

for shame
so strong
in thought

nowhere
to be found
a harbour
in the green leaves

(

)

Three blue plaques for Samuel Palmer

(At Shoreham)

Hung
in the world
the likeness of the world
decays beyond a likeness – dust
sticks to wet glaze – thus
to speak the truth
we idealise
slightly.

(At Leith Hill)

First
the nodding corn
and then the gleaners of the fields –
and there are fewer of them now
than once there were:
potent symbols.

(At Redhill)

Remember
that he barely went a day
without a backward look from Redhill
to Leith Hill to Shoreham, hopefully reflecting
there were hops after all in the gardens of Kent
exactly as I'd drawn before I went,
just as I doubted
after.

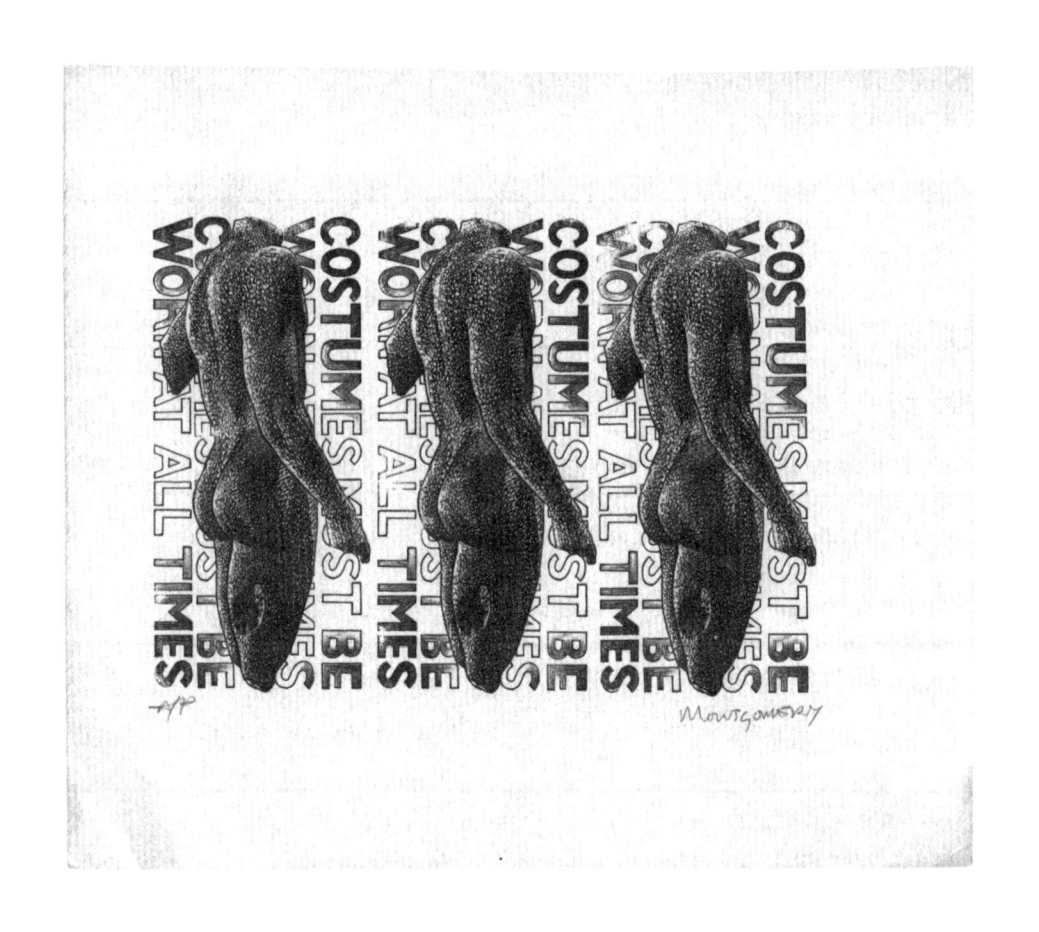

)

Jordan Hayward

—

The One with Ross's Teeth

The rumours of my death
have been greatly exaggerated
I am in full bloom
and will remain as such
until I expire
            even then
my cadaver will strike poses
glamorous poses
in the unrelenting fashion
of the moment

I will be wearing Ralph Lauren
      on my torso
my figure cradled by linen

My hair is so late night talk show
I can hardly believe it
even the barber was stunned
startled   admiring his handiwork
basically the modern day Michelangelo

I will wear Ralph Lauren on my legs
and compete in various Olympic games
      discus, archery, javelin
the main projectile sports
true athleticism

I will be designer
in my movements
      designer
on the podium

I will represent the Ralph Lauren brand
to the best of my ability

I will swim the length of the Seine
in a polo shirt and khakis

I will emerge at Côté Ouest Ormeaux
barely even wet

The One with the Routine

Finally my sheets were satin
my worries   heard and validated
my electric toothbrush burnished
with I think   sequins

Yes   even my dreams
changed perspective
I was an opulent ballroom
chandeliered   with all the fixings

They're all inside me, dancing!

Attempts at ejecting my denizens
are ineffective
                their frolic persists
despite my grouching
inhabited   as a prenatal womb

Their silhouettes   nice I suppose
cycloning   limbs aflurry
my freshly-waxed floor
subject to it all
glistening like precum

)

The One with the Apothecary Table

The white wine
refuses to spill
that's red's racket
       and its turf
shan't be encroached on

Fate   as you know
is a cowboy
with a pliant lasso
cattle tally declining
bolo tie slack and steely

Is no soirée complete
without misery
doled out bountifully
like canteen soup?

Or someone incorrectly naming
the small plates *chips and dips?*

I hope the light catches my scarf
(which is   of course   made of pearls)
and blinds them   coolly
in a way that implies it's their fault
for looking at my pearlscarf   uninvited

Honestly

Most of these guests
are welcome as hornets
in the quiche

Who could be that careless
perfectly   careless
flapping hands wielding glasses
of Château Margaux

I should contact my publicist
before commenting further
enact an embargo
on open carry of liquids
in future

Someone   please
fetch the baking soda
sharpish

You know
in days of yore
I could have had them
launched from a trebuchet
which seems an appropriate
amount of comeuppance

Your eyes snipe mine
from across the room
with a not wholly insincere
compassion revival look
that says *people are staring*

I holster my vengeance
for the time being   begrudgingly

Though please don't push me
by making jokes
                about the spillage
I will break out my harp
play something indescribably moving
and you will be forced to listen

Fuck it
        I can't stop looking

It's like an entire person
has been liquified on my chaise
morphed into their wettest version

I should buy a trebuchet
or   I don't know   a ballista

In the post-banquet photos
I will be flexed   taut
the ominous stance
of a wet floor sign

You will be unbothered
carefree as a taskless Sim
ever so soignée
in leopard

)

Jordan Hayward

The One Where Ross Meets Elizabeth's Dad

This is the time of year
you know it well
where even the cynics
astrologically speaking
depetal their skepticism

People will believe anything

To me   even iron
is a precious metal

In the faux-Scandi café
I looked into her mouth
waited for the coffee stains
to settle
            on her tongue
until they were as legible
as tea leaves

(

I pre-empted her verses
from the top
                this proved
highly generative

I've written fourteen books
following this method

My latest   *Long Pig*
is the jubilant chorus
to my career's song

One review stated *Long Pig*
was *the novel to end all novels*

Another called it *life-affirming*
        poignant
                a real Tour de France

I've had to employ
my pet falcon   Horus
to help me cope
        to sift
through the fan-mail

This new dynamic
has drastically altered
our relationship
    and as such
he no longer sees me
as his father

Various publications
reported that *Long Pig*'s audiobook
its Portuguese translation
        specifically
woke a Brazilian man
from a yearlong coma

Upon waking
he asked for a mixologist
to visit his bedside
        to prepare
celebratory caipirinhas
garnished with lime wheels
for him and his family

He enjoyed the cocktail
    to such a degree
that he forewent
the pageantry et cetera
and headed straight
for the bottle

)

The cachaça
according to eyewitnesses
was chugged
with such tenacity
that he died
        elatedly
on the spot

I maintain my book
was responsible
    solely
for waking him
not for the newfound
    lust for life
        party-loving spirit
that led to his death

Really   a doctor
should have stepped in

Perhaps I'm overreacting

On the Utrecht leg
of my book tour
a fortune-teller
predicted my teeth
would turn to rust
thanks to excessive consumption
of slow-brewed coffee
the finest
          of Yirgacheffes

I hid the bulk of myself
behind the lectern
shuffled pages to distract
though the barbs
kept coming

                    Apparently
(I was due to be overcharged
      for a taxi   suffer a mass-shrinking
      at the launderette
                    acquire an incurable
      urinary tract infection

I surmised this fortune-teller
had unresolved childhood trauma
          and was projecting

Everybody does this

Filled doughnuts
reaching into themselves
pulling out handfuls
of jam   seeds and all
to share with their ringèd comrades

I'm the target   clearly
of a vast and sprawling
CIA misinformation scheme

This thing goes right to the top

Many lovers' spats
followed my acclaim
this was to be expected

What wasn't expected
was the gladiatorial combat
           that followed
the not-unloving maiming
of a relationship

I didn't allow myself time
to mourn   I learned
how to put Horus' hair
into plaits   got close
to being able to speak
in his mother tongue
        fluently

I got my flâneur on
ordered café au lait
        croissants
sat overlooking the Seine
sipped observed
ate individual cornflakes
from a silver tray

        If the wind
blew me the right way
I'd flick one down to the rats
and place bets with myself
on which ones got to eat

In terms of her
I kept myself
        in the dark
thinking too much
left me chaise-bound
            powerless
watching reruns on cable
being fed hummus and cucumber
by Horus   still as a cadaver
easing into an embalming table

Only the scent
of Chanel No.5

Jordan Hayward

on my Ralph polo
had a calming
effect on me

I started clambering
into surging Ubers
saying things like
step on it   *full throttle*
          or
              follow that car
towards no car in particular
just for the thrill

I started bringing my own
pickled axolotl to restaurants

At the Chopin concerto
I was recognised
          of course I was
by a group of art students

(

I gave them each a twenty
told them to follow their dreams

Regardless
                time flies

In the backseat of a Benz
I'm verging on immortality

The driver knows this
that's why he offered me mints

Matthew Halliday

—

from *Revelations*

I took a long and slow sip of the glass of water in front of me, noting, as the water went slowly down my throat, that I wasn't thirsty, and that there wasn't any new information on the BBC news website. A deep primordial groan, as if from two colliding seismic plates, came shuddering out of the walls, before resolving itself into a semi-human squeal. The sound filled the office and cut right through my focus. I wondered what its origin was. It was low and echoing, as if coming from the internal plumbing, consisting of old lead pipes no doubt, carrying water or gas, or now redundant pipes that used to carry something and now just remained where they once had sense to be. Something in the building was expanding or buckling under the incredible heat.

    The website in front of me was famished for tragedy, it badly wanted news to break and for that news to be enormous, impossible. I too was feverishly awaiting crises in my boredom, crises that were expected to unfold soon and appear in news reports, incidents that were surely certain to occur on the third day of this heatwave, due to be the hottest so far. For now, it seemed we were in the eye of the storm. I – we – were waiting. A cartoon thermometer was bouncing up and down on the page. It was annoying me – lots of things were annoying me. Whose creation was this? Too cheerful tech-evangelists no doubt, the only people in our society who looked optimistically towards the future. It was infantilising, toxic positivity, and I did not like it. The temperature was currently at the previous day's high, which had been the hottest day of the year. No tragedies or disasters had yet made themselves known below the headline.

    I had been trying and failing to browse the page in front of me. Although I could see the words, I was failing to squeeze out their meaning. I closed my eyes, wiped some sweat from around my eye-sockets – thoroughly, languidly – and opened them once more, this time hoping to be able to digest the contents. There were at least two articles explaining the pollution warning that had been issued, what the various types of harmful particles that were in the air were, the threats they carried to human health and what were the premier causes of each one. It had only been in the last year or so that pollution levels in London had been regularly referenced in the media. The incipient hysteria was constrained, for now, to make room for reports on the growing list of train stations and airports that had to close for reasons relating to the heat. I stared passively at the self-refreshing page as new bullets appeared, simultaneously carrying the prosaic traffic information and their allusive proper nouns, hauling medieval baggage into the motionless present. Kings Cross St Pancras has been closed. Charing Cross and Euston have been closed since 10:30. All planes have been grounded at Stansted and Gatwick pending further updates. Mary-le-bone has been closed. No trains are running through Blackfriars.

The first time I'd read about pollution in the air in any detail had also been on the BBC website. The article had been about the smog that blighted Beijing, and had been marbled with Sinophobia, discernible in the offhand observations that spiced the common-sense journalist's otherwise neutral prose. Recently I'd even read a story about trade deal discussions between the US and China that had begun: 'Over the metallic sheen of Beijing's polluted skies…', as if that had any relevance to the negotiations. Pollution was apparently an Eastern problem, and a moral one at that, a problem of shame, an inescapable stain of progress and destruction that poured into the lungs of expendable labour overseas. The workshop of the world had migrated east. Those upstart Chinese communists had the gall to morph into capitalists, was there anything communism wasn't capable of? At some point, though, the dialogue about climate change seemed to have changed, presumably around the same time that the fair-play United Kingdom began to experience extreme weather conditions with increasing frequency. Now, the problem seemed existential. The problem seemed to be disconcertingly real.

Nowadays, each summer, every news source included reports of what had become annual flooding of various low-lying towns across the country – Gloucester, Ironbridge or York or wherever it might be. It tended to be older, historically significant settlements that were especially vulnerable to being swallowed up by rising water levels, but it wasn't just these sites of dim memories. The previous decade had also seen a building boom on flood-plains, with the major building contractors seemingly making most of their money selling these quickly to uninformed members of the public, with plenty of government encouragement. A fresh scandal for the future. How much of the old and new would be washed away, and how soon? I wondered if the papers reporting the Chinese smog, the yellow peril, would have registered the same shock and disapproval if they had seen one of the infamous London smogs materialise again, such as the so-called Great Smog of 1952. An atmosphere so opaque and fatal parliament hurriedly pushed through the Clean Air Act in direct response, banning coal fires from London. Coal fires had heated homes in this city for perhaps a thousand years, powering the expansion of this anachronistic behemoth. No more. I could feel my temples pulsing. I took another slow sip of my unwanted glass of water.

 What a hot conundrum we were in, what would the pitiless future bring? For now, despite the pre-emptively gloating front page, no news was forthcoming, and we were left to speculate and wait for further announcements. I sat, semi-shielding my screen from the others, although everyone else in the office seemed to be dithering around much as I was: listlessly scrolling along the narrow corridors of the BBC website, waiting for some drama to unfold in the distant elsewhere and deliver something that would hold our attention. It was as if my body had become enshrouded by smog and I was now weightless and invisible. I could feel my thoughts untethering, floating through a network of unknown canals, at mercy to their architecture, at mercy to mysterious currents. Connection-less, direction-less. I could see nothing significant in the present world I was in.

 This was my approach to the boredom that had begun to occupy me in today's mid-afternoon slump, regular as the seasons and here once again on this impossibly hot, humid and grey September afternoon that no one was pleased to find themselves in. There were three desk fans feebly spinning away on each desk, each trying to coax the hot air around the room with exhausted whirrs, some of the very few ornaments of the spartan office. I was sat at one of the four desks. There were three other equally-bored-seeming occupants, and otherwise nothing but obsolete office miscellany. It was only in the unbearable heat that I'd really clocked the latter. What was in those anonymous filing cabinets? And the grubby books on the shelf above my desk, what use for anyone did they have? And come to think of it there was little reason for all the reams of paper in untidy piles either. I looked more closely at them. Each one had a proudly stamped header celebrating imperial power: a lion walking upright on its spindly legs as if in a circus act, the mythical unicorn opposite, rearing upwards. Both tightly hugged a shield, a crown.

I'd never properly examined the headers before. They were a sign that every recipient would immediately recognise and yet did not see. From His Majesty, that is, via the Civil Service. One drawer of my desk was full of this headed paper, which had lain there untouched the entire time I'd worked here, at least three years. Why was all this stuff lying around? Perhaps someone realised that if they removed all the detritus it would reveal the office to be completely empty of anything at all, and although no one had been moved to make this space lovelier than it was, they drew the line at revealing it to be the cell it really was, painted in creaking antiseptic green. Things that had once seemed practical and essential persisted into times where they were not. Most of what composed our environment, our world, were things that no longer served a function, things that nobody cared for. They refused to be seen until they were sorely missed.

I stared upwards at the redundant clock: 3:30. Its big hand was heavy and slow, even the twitching second hand seemed to be moving begrudgingly. I sat there staring at the hands for a few moments – they clicked a dozen or so times – then I looked away. This was unbearable. I was severely bored: every moment felt like a throb.

These were the times when my mind started to wander around the room. What is in that desk, what are those piles of paper for? How do things relate and coincide? How many hours had I spent dithering around in this office and in this chair? Too many to count. The desperate refuge of the profoundly bored: the why question – what is this scenery, what brought this situation about, what is the history? On examination the world would seem to silt up, become cluttered and full. I became fixated on the way things used to be. The different flavour in the air that had brought them into being, this building too, this city, this society. The more stuck my body was in its present reality, the more my consciousness seemed to wander off into a dream. They were dreams dressed in the garb of previous times, with different ways of looking, different ways of doing things. Fixated, enraptured, captivated, I drank the strangeness that these dreams brought like narcotic honey.

    I craved this special receptive state, I yearned to be haunted. I'd had afternoons stretch into evenings, where I'd just sat here dreaming, wondering. Usually something would jolt me out of it, and then the thoughts would evaporate, until I had no memory of what exactly they'd been. The smell of them seemed to linger in the air like a recently extinguished candle: exotic, foreign, irresistible, but also intangible, unlocatable. Did everyone experience such things? Maybe they did, but I seemed to be more susceptible than most. Looking backwards, yearning for something gone. It was socially disapproved of, it seemed, because it was unproductive. What was the use of staring at crests and postmarks? Society was not interested in this utility-less information. The signs of previous times were actively unperceived, like old-fashioned wallpaper, or a left-on radio. Too allusive, too question-begging, too much.

)

Angélica Pina Lèbre

What is she to me?

She's missing, I told them. They asked me questions. I answered them. They asked me if I had

a picture, I pulled out my phone and showed them a photo. *What is she to you?* the policeman

asked. I didn't know what to say.

I eventually left the police station and went back to the house. I was hopeful she might have

found her way back home. She hadn't. The house was empty. I went to her bedroom, lay on her

bed, burrowed my nose in her pillow.

Laced in smoky lavender I inhaled her nonenal smell.

(

What is she to you? What is she to me?

She's my everything.

My mother. My father.

My son. My daughter.

My sister. My brother.

My wife. My husband.

My friend.

136

Jack Young

—

**TUMBA TYMBUS TOMBA
TOMBA T'UMB TOMM TOMBE**

in the archaeological museum in athens/wandering between   *Andreas*
tomba/tumba/tomb/*soft ruins*/stone/seeming/fixed/   *Angelidakis*
shifting/beneath naked eyes

in the archaeological museum in athens/lusting for
tomba/tymbus/tombe/naked torsos/marble-smooth/erect
at the point of eruption/erect/at the peak of war

in the archaeological museum in athens/in the sixth room
(((of thirty)))/i notice an insect in the/so-called/sterile
case/creeping across the chiselled nipple of apollo

in the archaeological museum in athens/yearning for
tombe/tumba/t'umb/bug body/delicately/poised/   )
bug/meaning/out of sight/meaning/disgust/meaning/how
us boys/fumbled thru the restless nights

in the archaeological museum in athens/i see the creatures   *Howard*
wings/new structures entire/a feature *shared only with*   *Ensign*
angels*/this bug-angel/roaming the ripped torso of apollo   *Evans*
s/s/s/s/mothering with excess

in the archaeological museum in athens/in the ninth room   *sarx: flesh*
((of thirty-five))/i dream of tymbus/tombe/t'umb/   *phagein:*
sarcophagus/meaning/limestone/meaning/flesh-   *to eat*
eating/meaning/the night he said/his body/
marble-stone-strong/was collapsing

in the archaeological museum in athens/searching vast
hallways of ancient tumba/tombe/tomba/lion gate of
acropolis/mycenae/ruminating/ruins we leave behind/what
legacies usher across ever-parched earth

Jack Young

in the archaeological museum in athens/in the twelfth room (((of fifty)))/black & white photographs/ruins/excavated a century before/lush fern tongues lick limestone slabs/refound/hand-in-hand in the thicket/crew-cut sister & me/wearing mothers clothes/bug-angels fluttering thru the frame

in the archaeological museum in athens/next to the photographs/a t'umb/tomb/tombe/sarcophagus/called attium/or something similar/journal smudged/phone picture blurred/only fragments left/*a conversation between what is broken*

Terry Tempest Williams

in the archaeological museum in athens/the sarcophagus attium/atrium/atheneum/attic/as in the region around athens/attic/as in the place we hid together as kids/when the adult-blue voices got too loud/downstairs

(

in the archaeological museum in athens/the attic sarcophagus/figure reclined/from the neck down/female/male-appearing/head/stone bodies/combined/the family reused the same sarcophagus/twice/economic difficulties/in death/maybe/especially/we reconstruct our bodies/time & time again

in the archaeological museum in athens/standing in front of the stone chimera/evidence how even/perhaps especially/stones shift/geological cataclysms/move with their own temporalities/the limestone/molten/melding of the earth

in the archaeological museum in athens/i think of my father's tombe/tymbus/tomb/two months after burial/sarcophagus barely flesh-eaten/bones emerging/tongue still rolling in his mouth/oesophagus communing with tree roots underground/bug-angels flickering into life/antennae stroking still-warm skin

in the archaeological museum in athens/two months after
burial/the tomb/tombe/tymbus was missing/missed/
vanished/strange/looking for tomb/t'umb/tomba/
not transformed/like attic sarcophagus/but gone/
blood-red holly/yew needles splayed/the gap/
where the stone had been

in the archaeological museum in athens/i remember he died
with too much debt/to pay for his tomb/tomba/tymbus/&
his wife/had kept this a secret/like attic sarcophagus/our
economic difficulties meant we could not afford the grave

in the archaeological museum in athens/i feel a kinship/with
the attic/athenian/attium/atrium/sarcophagus/forced by
economic hardship into/reusing busts & bodies/merged/to
maintain the stone memory/though the stone/so soon/
softening

in the archaeological museum in athens/in the thirty-first
room ((((of one hundred))))/i remember going missing/like
my father from his stone/unsure where to locate my
body/& desires/as he collapsed into the earth

)

in the archaeological museum in athens/the attic
sarcophagus moving so playfully between forms/shifting
beyond a monolith of death/& gender/never as stable as we
think/playful hack & glitch stone/re-etched with
openings/& possibilities

in the archaeological museum in athens/in the fifty-second
room (((of one hundred & sixty))) i think of my fathers
body/& desires/the slamming of doors/to our bodies/&
our desires/huddled together/abandoned in the house
moon-blue

in the archaeological museum in athens/when i die/i want
my tomb/tumbe/tymbus to keep switching heads/to

Jack Young

reconstruct my stone-body/again & again/to glitch & hack/my form/left behind

in the archaeological museum in athens/when i die/i want my tomb/tombe/tumba/to be smothered in bug-angels/ lichen-fucked/throbbing with excessive earth-clotted rot/glass cases cracking open/*the asshole a lichen thallus/a bright new dream*/leichen/ lichen/λειχήν/eruption on skin & stone

declan wiffen

in the archaeological museum in athens/when i die/i will speak in fossil-tongues/soil-whispering/secret languages beyond museum ears/beyond the living/the dead/beyond the dead/enlivening/new ghosts

in the archaeological museum in athens/in the two-hundredth room (((of five thousand)))/i find my father's tomb/tymbus/t'umb/covered in moss/leichen-devoured/the face of the boy we once were/& the body of a bug-angel/wings/f

(

/

c   e   ̀

̀

k   r   n

&

—
Andreas Angelidakis, *Soft Ruins* installation as part of the exhibition 'Modern Love (or Love in the Age of Cold Intimacies)' at EMST: National Museum of Contemporary Art Athens, Summer 2023

Howard Ensign Evans, *Life on a Little-Known Planet* (Andrew Deutsch, 1966)

Terry Tempest Williams, *Finding Beauty in a Broken World* (Vintage, 2009)

Declan Wiffen, from 'symbiosis or ass & lichen for Sol LeWitt' in *SPAM005*, www.spamzine.co.uk/spam005

Rochelle Roberts

—

from *Divination*

FAMILY PORTRAIT

I.
I become a site of memory, a touchstone for the retention of past trauma. The picture is clear, like a photograph, except it is not what was seen but what was felt.

II.
In the memory, my father wears a black suit, tobacco smoke lining the creases of his white shirt. He can't open his eyes, his head slumped forward as if he were sleeping, or dead, or unknown and unknowable. I cannot look into his face, so I hold his hand and lean my head against his arm – an intimacy that lingers in my peripheral vision. I remember his small hand in mine and how soft it feels, the same kind of soft as my grandmother's hand which I sat holding after she had died. I wondered, at the time, how death could have made her so edgeless, so unlike herself. I had a strong desire to photograph her hand, her face, her bruised arm, but somehow it felt improper or disrespectful. I needed to commit the image of her to memory, the way Alice Neel painted her father on his deathbed from memory, the way she painted her daughter from memory after she was taken away. The memory of loss as clear as a photograph, my phone camera a useless and invasive tool. The picture is clear.

Because my father could not open his eyes while he sat with me, it was as if I had lost him for a moment.

A hard lump formed in my throat.

The skin on my father's hand had a blue tinge, a very specific shade, like the way it feels to dissolve perpetually into empty space. I knew that a line of blue reached up the inside of his arm, up across his shoulder and down his spine. He called it *La Marafona*. The edges of

the line blistered in the same way watercolour fractures in water.
I often ran my finger along this line. It reminded me of Alice's electric blue, except my father's blue did not hold the same signs of life. Once, I thought I could turn his blue electric, by being a better daughter, by performing acts of care. He told me he often dreamed in blue light, that everything he experienced was the sound and shape of *La Marafona*.

III.
In the memory, it is the last time I can think of that my father still remembered his name.

IV.
My mother did not understand. In her not-understanding she became grotesque. What I knew of her was her short, gloved fingers pressing into my father's shoulders. She couldn't keep him upright. In the memory, she had put on her red lipstick, had dressed in an elaborate burnt orange dress that made her look too large, too unwieldy. The lipstick had smudged at the edges, stained her teeth, but I could not bring myself to tell her; I felt too far away. It is this difference, of my mother being alive to what happened in the world while my father slowly disappeared, that kept her fleshy. She moved through space with a fluidity that I could not comprehend, and it made her all the more strange to me. It was as if she existed in a reality that my father and I could not penetrate. She breathed in air, and we breathed in that perpetual blue, *the colour of our dreams.*

V.
I sat with my father and tried not to imagine him dead.

LOSS OF SELVES

I.
There is something about the inheritance of disorder, a lineage
of unwellness, the language of loss.

My father had a sister. There is a photograph of them when they are
maybe three or four years old. They are standing in the garden of the
home where they grew up, in London. They look like twins, each with
identical outfits, identical hairstyles. My aunt places a hand on my
father's shoulder as if to comfort him – the perpetuity of keeping
him upright. He looks frightened.

I asked him what had troubled him. Why was it that he looked so
worried, so sad for such a young child. He told me the photograph had
been taken not long after his family had arrived in London. They had
had to leave their home because of disaster. A mountain of ash had
buried their house, along with every other house on that part of the
island, every building, every tree, every road. Erased as if it was
never there.

My father could not metabolise his grief, he could not keep it in.
It spilled across the surface of the photograph, across the surface
of his life, trickled down through the crevices and cracks like ash,
like water.

I made a copy of that photograph to stick to my bedroom wall, to
remember what it had cost to exist in a place that did not belong
to you.

I later thought of it as the beginning of blue, the inciting incident that
caused *La Marafona* to bruise into my father's skin. Perhaps he realised
it too. Maybe that is why eventually he took a paintbrush and cocooned
himself and my aunt in watery white acrylic paint. Parts of them
showed through the uneven layer of paint. My father's sad expression
took on a haunted look.

It felt to me like a destruction of what had been, a time that was difficult but one that they had survived. Yet, I started to wonder whether that was not my father's intention, that he no longer wanted the evidence of loss. Because it was not only their home that was gone, they had lost themselves or what they would have been had they been able to stay.

They were *not here, not there, neither here nor there, elsewhere.*
They were *somewhere else, nowhere, no place, absent.*

II.
Before the blue took him, my father often spoke of my aunt. They had evacuated their island home with their parents, found themselves in a small ground-floor flat in North London with cracked walls, mould spores and a small garden to breathe in. The disorientation of moving brought them closer together. Their minds developed a kind of synchronicity, so that they often dreamed collectively. They became so insular that my grandparents understood them less and less.
They became grotesque.

My father would tell me about trying to navigate the world through difference – that his and my aunt's difference was so obvious to them that they began to believe they were of another place, not merely distinct because of ethnicity, culture, language, but because they were fundamentally alien, other. My grandparents wanted them to slip seamlessly into their new roles as Londoners, but they did not know how. My father would tell me these things and I would think how strange it must have been, as strange as it would be for me to be forced to move to his island home and make a life for myself there. He told me it was not only the material things that made a difference. It was the way the air smelled and tasted different. The way the ground felt beneath his feet. It was how the birds sounded or the fact that many of the creatures, trees, flowers, scents that he knew were missing.

He and my aunt dreamed of home endlessly until they could not dream any more.

III.
In the memory of my father, he was perfumed with blue. His hand was so small, like a child's. After this memory, he collapsed and never got up again. He'd forgotten his name.

When my aunt was young, younger than I am now, she fell and was crushed against the pavement. She never got up again.

My father could not get up for months. He lay in bed and did not speak, not even to my mother who started sleeping with me, only entering her bedroom to bring my father small plates of food. I would slip into their bedroom when my father was asleep, just to sit on the floor by the bed and look at him. I would stare hard and hope that by fixing my eyes on his face I could will him back to life. A copy of Roland Barthes's *Mourning Diary* sat immovably on his bedside table, the pages folded at the corners so that the book would not lay flat. He had underlined and circled various sentences in red ink, and sometimes, when I was alone in my room, I would recite them quietly as though they were incantations ~

)

How strange: her voice, which I knew so well, and which is said to be the texture of memory...

Does being able to live without someone you loved mean you loved them less than you thought...?

~ and I felt as if the words bridged the gap of his absence as they moved through the air.

IV.
I wanted to understand why what had happened had happened.
My mother could not tell me, so I had to find out for myself.

I tried to enter my father's dreams the way my aunt could, but he would not let me in.

I tried to listen as he stared out of the window, but he would not let me in.

I tried to enter his body through osmosis, but he would not let me in.

V.
It took an inordinately long time for him to start to leave his bedroom. Even after he did, I was aware very quickly that he was changed. He moved with less precision, took longer to respond during conversation. Slowly, over time, he forgot things. It was after my aunt died that *La Marafona* appeared on his skin. My mother never said anything about it. I was unsure whether she had noticed or cared. She was different too. She began to leave the house for long periods of time – I think, simply to get away from my father. She never told me where she was going and always made sure her phone was off so we couldn't contact her. Before leaving, she would make food for my father which she put in the oven covered with tin foil until he was ready to attempt eating it. Most of the time, he only ate a few mouthfuls, and I ate the rest.

I did not try to understand my mother because I had no desire to. At times I found it hard to believe we had once been connected, that I had existed within her body. How was it I had grown inside of her, but I could not dissolve through my father's skin, I could not get past that stubborn barrier.

VI.
I have now lost the photocopied version of the photograph. Only the defaced original remains. I look at it often, running my fingers over its uneven surface or holding it to my chest as if I may at last join my father's and aunt's collective unconscious. Somehow the picture is even more melancholy, even more haunted. I no longer think of it as a testament to survival. Instead, it is an emblem of loss.

Maya Uppal
–
from *Museum = Time Machine*

Notes from the First Day

the museum is little nation

your new nation!
your new border!

post-written by academic hangovers
all the post-grads are tender headed
talking about the queasy feeling of
being spat out of the course
into semi-permanent contracts
they're the bodies who fill the space

have you noticed that box yet?   )
the one oozing back into the walls?

it's the turrets you want to avoid
shelves on the edge of collapse
what's that word? oh yeah,
microcosm

one lecture too few to address it
there's no time once you've
neutralised the present
presented the present
as wrapped in pasts
ignored the past as if
wrapped in futures

the time machine forgets who built it
after a certain number of years in action

Maya Uppal

ignore the archive melting off the shelves
the museum is never too crowded!
its walls reinforce borders
glass cases leave you stateless
but now, back to our post-grads

the you that leaves will
not be the you who arrived

(

Case Study: Collecting the Once Living and the Now Dead

I find her/my cranium alone. in the box alongside three others. the cranium is alone, I should say, in relation to the rest of her/my body.

her/my bone was a gift

the skull indicates a historic person. here we're not talking about bone/flesh/organs. but thoughts/memories/life. it is natural to wonder, to recollect, the bone into flesh into organ into thought into feeling into memory into costume into ritual into survival into stories into guesswork.

as I write my report, I compare the lesions on the exposed bones to the imperfections of mine. in missing teeth and fractured lines, I hide mundane truths and allow the patch-work stories of conservationists to smooth themselves into reality. this once-brained rock is left all scrubbed up. preserved and under watch, almost removed from her/my history of muscle of organs of growth, this bone has become hand-fixed. visually-storied.

)

where the once-bodied may have been consecrated or discarded at any moment the absence of full skeletal remains indicates, as I view her/my cranium only, the years of neglect her/my bones have endured and continue to endure.

so, take the person

ignore, for a moment, her/my condition of preservation. examine the contours of her/my jaw for signs of grinding. find our missing teeth in the bottom of the box, wrapped in our own tissue paper. acid – free. notice, how bone, is treated like rock, is treated like fossils.

I consider taking the skull-rock as a votive offering for her/my future museum. I considered allowing her/my skull to become another missing thing.

in her/my

Maya Uppal

skull/rock

I find a placeholder

a container for illusory worlds. before the shelves were built, trapping all their big ideas in rotting boxes. I considered a return to earth. she asks, is a return to earth enough?

bring your ethnology into the room

allow the bone to pretend it has been cast aside rather than taken. protect the skull from the zoological and racial characteristics that have been assigned to its form. decipher the label to tell me if her/my skull is Asian/South Asian/ Native American/Polynesian/Middle Eastern/African/ another invented sticking place. Realise that missing origins, gifted origins, looted origins, found origins, are meaningfully applied to her/my skull as a non-white collectible object in a European Museum.

(bring your ethnology into the room

realise that her/my skull is a tool for the mapping of racial classification theories onto collections of human remains. realise that classifications of bone were attempts to make visible race as physically indicated post-death and post-culture. realise that the separation of skull from body from culture from burial has resulted in spiritual sickness. haunted boxes. diseased inaction.

so, take the object

my/her momentum is activated by the fluorescent switch. the teasing storage pods. I/she is punished by the time it takes to contemplate their numbers. We make our decision but take no time to wonder if liberation for the object (as I view it) through the act of stealing is to confine her/my skull to another prison, this time of our own making.

shrines gather up their conceptual ideals

laden with practical flaws and veiled data

I am left to make up stories

which should be left to decompose

in one moment, I'll open the box to reveal that her/my skull is gone

the soul that is mine has been taken already

)

Maya Uppal

Thieving Dreaming Ritual

in the beginning not mentioning the missing *(read: lost)*
was a fireable offence yet to witness a grand disappearance
I practise fantasies of re-looting and I take *(read: need)*
whatever fits in my pocket gods charms shells cups jewellery
the ephemeral signals of lives lived outside of this room *(read: country)*
I've been seeking the small stuff geographically speaking
I don't think nature would mind being taken into my grimy verses
any more than notice how my curators have taken

    is not the preferred term of my curator
    gifted holds court in her throat
    gifted jumps into the mouths of
    the others quickly, who follow suit
    to tell me they have noticed
    how my trips to the lockers
    have grown more frequent

(

the missing *(read: found)*
gather all the nonsense meanings I've stuck to them
learn quickly that no eye can watch all objects at once
learn to not mention the missing *(read: unidentified)*
to miss you must first value what was taken
who, before me, had forgotten *(read: deliberately ignored)*
the box room for every object I repatriate back
into my own pocket is missing *(read: experiencing traumatic loss)*
I trawl the shelves for new histories to devour
in the bristling presence of Objective Limbo
until the missing *(read: rehomed)*
site is spotted years days minutes later

Time Travel is just Another Word for Spatial Desire

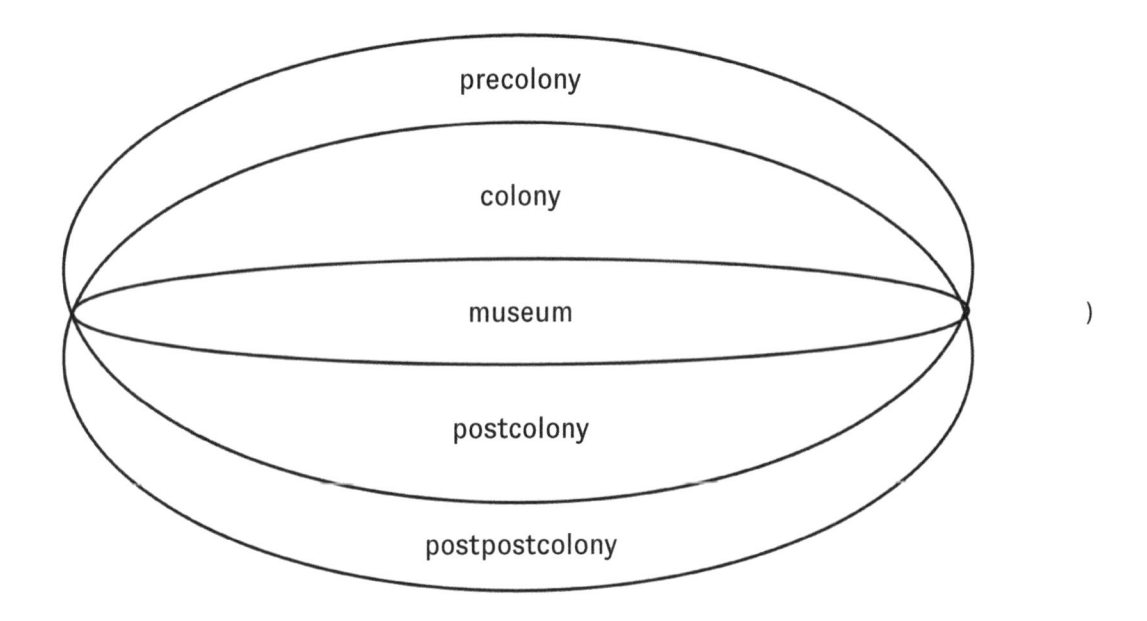

precolony

colony

museum

postcolony

postpostcolony

)

c.f. prior

—

Delaying, lingering, residing: an essay in four rooms

I — *delaying, lingering, residing*

I pass a sunken week. I can't draw the things I want to draw nearer to me nearer to me and you are getting further away. More or less a year after his death, you find you can no longer find the name or memory you are looking for when you go looking for it. And you are getting lost outside of language too. New plate glass parts unfold from the old city to make a maze of your map. You keep turning up on the doorstep of your previous life. Cops call to tell me you became distressed on a bus travelling to nowhere I have ever known you to go. In my mind two red eyes close around a corner and I find myself wondering who lived where along the route. So ten years after he first entered the scanner, I take you. We're in the antechamber to a new life. I don't want to do what I know I have to do for a second time. I want to be heliotropic in the park forever, a little radar open to the premature season's gifts, on for everyone, beneath the wet trees, delicate pink cyclamen unfurling at my feet. Instead I step backwards over the threshold into the structure of the life we temporarily shared and am enveloped by lily of the valley *green, clean, wholesome, fresh and optimistic as the morning dew* the sales copy says. It's lodged in my mind as the fragrance of my tenancy in the framework of someone else's desire. I used to finger loose filaments in the sisal, watch rain drops vie for pole position down the pane and, up with the insomniac pigeons, the planes' landing lights hoovering up the night, and plan my egress from the situation, try to slide sideways out of it like a letter pushed beneath a door. around the table with sarah and deirdre from the older people community mental health team my eyes rest on the cobalt oxide foliage in the decorative delft chinoiserie wall plates. It looked benign, like lichen or a rorschach test, in the images.

(

II — *holding, keeping, grasping*

As hard as you push against your new cohabitant, your new cohabitant pushes against the parameters of physics—gifts you the symptom of time travel and makes everywhere *terra nullius*. When someone interprets your attempt to return as squatting you protest. Say: *this is my home.* I get a text about this so long I have to read more. Like something caught in the throat, you get dislodged into the drawing room of someone who winters as a verb, where I visit you once. On the red damask sofa surrounded by someone else's belongings you look out of place, a mispick in the weave. Here, caught in a holding pattern, circling inside someone else's possession, we've arrived at the moment when the weft of your fantasy has failed to interlace with the warp of your reality. Untethered from the blueprint of your dream life you become to all around you an unwanted forecast; you start to signal disturbance.
Did Lot's decision not to turn and bear witness minimise the damage? In the moment of their turning away they create a copula between you and me. In the closed loop of someone else's single family home, I am—*in the end*—your child.
⠀⠀⠀)

III — *supplying, adjusting, accommodating*

Caught in the rectilinear logic of your local borough's housing allocation process the circumstances of your loss are transmuted into data to be analysed, rated and mapped. Natural as interest rates and dividends, a table on the webpage documents the decline in social housing units across the borough over the past decade. One thousand six hundred and fifty two properties hungering for inhabitants. I note on the table when and where the number of available social housing units drops precipitously. When finally you accrue enough points to be temporarily housed in supported accommodation clad in multicoloured risk, it's not possible to forget why. I rode my bike to see you and didn't get there until spring. You wouldn't let me in. The city was folded over itself like an envelope: benches threaded with caution tape, the bathrooms everywhere locked up. You needed my help to renew your bus pass but I couldn't do it without the forms you didn't yet want to sign. One day c.f. prior

like a day, a dream, a government this'll all be over. Homeward bound the sun is skims every surface in the city. Light spreads over it all like a blood orange squeezed out.

IV — *resting, hosting, waiting*

On hold to the care home, the social worker, the office of the public guardian, whoever, I pray for the screeching aerobatics of the swifts overhead. Tiny scythes tilting in the sun. I'm tired of being on hold. A whole year at half-mast. Every time I call I get a different answer, what do you do when you can do nothing? Already alert, I lace myself with caffeine. Faced with the consequences of someone else's unplanned future, I'm compelled to plan for my own. I'm getting ready to peacock. I'm getting ready to go outside. I'm building muscle, I'm restoring furniture—sanding it back, working oil and wax into the grooves with a former T-shirt—I'm learning French again. All this against all that. Outside the barber sweeps up commas of hair. Spills out with the last customers onto the street. Past all those partitions, cleaving, for you, interior from exterior, I visit you there on the underside of welcome.
In here I'm your *son the academic.* Someone's pocketed the photographs on your wall. Spread them around like communal recollection.
No uneven distribution in this the fragile economy of memory: we don't remember alone.

(

Kat Chimonides

—

from *On Feeling Seen*

The Art School

I'm with a textiles class and the students have been asked to bring clothes, fabrics, for me to wear. Colour, pattern, texture – the more expressive the better. I start with a few short poses, naked, then onto the outfits. From the pile I choose a fitted jacket and a headscarf. A student completes my look with her handmade wire waistcoat. As she's helping me into the structure, I notice the wire brushing against my pubes. Only now do I question how appropriate it is to be this close to a student whilst wearing nothing on my lower half. I think I'll wear pants in future classes. But bright ones, ones that will be interesting to look at and capture on paper.

On a day when there weren't many clothes to choose from, the tutor wheeled the rail of costumes out from the models' changing area. He taught differently to others, encouraging students not to measure or use pencils. By interpreting me in pen they would produce a more confident line. Somebody decided I should wear the white dress. Stood on a low block, I became a star of *My Big Fat Gypsy Wedding*. Mountains of mesh surrounded me. The class agreed I had been left at the altar.

*

The Painter's Studio

I am lying on a dust sheet beneath a coffee table. There are pieces of foam under the sheet to support my head, neck and lower back. We spent a while getting these in place, and each time I shuffle in and out of position, I try not to move them. The table, its white paint flaking, had been in the shed a long time. He dusted it down with a bit of cloth and I asked him to check for spiders. We laughed and I said I wouldn't be able to keep still if a spider fell on me. He said I would have to, that's what he's paying me for. We laughed again as he inspected the table, turning it over, brushing the cobwebs away.

From where he is standing, he can see my head, chest, arms, hands and toes. There is a heater near my left side. When he isn't painting my right hand, I wear a green chenille glove. If I forget to bring my gloves, I use one of my socks instead. If conversation lulls, or if I'm not following the radio talk, I sometimes fall asleep. He says he doesn't mind. Incredibly I'm able to stay in the pose. No twitching. Some dribbling, but he can't see that. In the middle of the table is a black plastic bucket. At first he put the table drawer on top, moved it around, painted it. Then he chose the bucket, painted over the drawer. We spoke for a short time about which looked better. One day I arrived and he'd painted over the bucket, the table was empty. Today marks the bucket's return. The timer goes off on his phone and we take a break. Once out from under the table I put on my dressing gown and socks, and I kneel in front of the wood burner on the other side of the studio. My eyes are moving between the scene and the painting. He is asking what I think. I smile and say there's a lot going on. What is the bucket doing? Bucket for water or ice, bucket and spade, mop and bucket, so bucket for cleaning. Building-site bucket for mixing cement, plaster. This bucket is cracked so it cannot contain. This bucket is dirty. But you have already painted this bucket with a shrub in it so this bucket can contain. This bucket is empty, waiting to be filled. Bucket as vessel, as woman. Sarah Lucas's bucket. He breathes out, exaggerating the puff of air as it leaves his mouth. So you like it then? I smile and nod. It's very layered. And the table, well, I'm being crushed by domesticity. He is smiling. But the table isn't touching you, you have plenty of room to escape. We both laugh at this and I head back to get into position.

    Sarah Lucas's bucket is crude, funny. It is metal, dented. Empty, this 3D object invites the viewer to look inside. It is a woman's inside which has been used repeatedly, made bigger. It gapes, an opening to be filled and that cucumber just won't do.

Last week I was on my period. I wore jogging bottoms to hide my sanitary towel wings. Even with the foam on the floor, I was in agony. I took extra breaks, apologised, and crouched with my back to the wood burner. After, on the bus, I couldn't sit up straight. I wrapped my coat around my bag and used it as a cushion, leaning at a diagonal and holding my belly. When I got home I curled on my bed and almost cried. The day's work hadn't been great for him either. The jogging bottoms raised my hips ever so slightly, which in turn shifted my upper half. When my period was over and I returned to the original position, what he saw didn't match what he had painted. He had to redo the entire section.

He is talking about the bucket's pouring lip, how it echoes the shape of my nose. He likes this aspect of the composition. He says he isn't too concerned with the objects' meanings or associations; he thinks they're suited. Table and bucket; bucket and table; table and woman and bucket; a woman, her bucket and a table. I ask why he often paints fragmented figures, and if he knows Erwin Wurm's *One Minute Sculptures*. Not paintings, I realise, but they're about bodies interacting with objects. He'll look them up. He says that although I know him for his portraits, he used to paint still-lifes. What he's working on now, these are still-lifes.

In the first painting he did of me, the coffee table is standing on its side. I'm lying on my back, the top third of me hidden. My right elbow, part of my right boob, my left hand and the rest of my body protrudes from between the table legs. The back of my right hand brushed the underneath corner of the table. I think of the strain on my armpit. How my hand would go cold, numb. Pins-and-needles ran the length of my arm. He is very good at capturing my feet, the way they turn in a little. They are distinctly mine. My ribs and hip bones jut out. Density is tangible in my thighs, my bum. One good thing about my head being hidden, I was able to change its position often. It also didn't matter if my eyes were open or closed. He and I chatted, the radio was on, or he played an audiobook. We laugh often. As someone who laughs with their body, I try hard to keep still and relatively quiet.

He asks if he can move some of my hair using the end of a paintbrush. It's fallen differently today and he can't see the lighter bits which he could yesterday. Apart from the first time we met when we shook hands, this is the closest we have come to touching. As I feel a brief, gentle sweep on the top of my head, I consider what we would be like together. This fantasy is short-lived, not because I feel guilty about cheating on my boyfriend or breaking up a marriage, but because I remember that he is a father. Due to my lack of maternal instinct I find this off-putting, so I instead think about what I've packed for lunch.

> Erwin Wurm relies on participants to manipulate their bodies. I became a shelf, clenching books in the spaces between my arms and my legs. My boyfriend stuck his head in a hole in the back of a sofa. We wore a jumper together, each putting one arm in one sleeve. I stood in a white plastic bucket whilst wearing a yellow plastic bucket on my head.

I am wiggling my fingers and toes, asking if I can move my neck. He says sure, go for it, and I slowly turn to face the ceiling, then to look towards the right, then back to the ceiling. I ask if the lights are new and he seems confused. They've been here since they converted the barn, a good while before I first came here. I say that's weird, I've never noticed them before. I move my head towards my chest, then back to the left. He asks if I can lift my head a tiny bit. Yeah, that's it. I'm facing the drawers again, with small frames stacked on top. Do you make all your own frames? He says he does, mostly. All the large ones, some of the small ones. We talk about the differences between making your own and buying them. It's all about the quality of the canvas. We've spoken before about art school, how I used to paint using acrylics but never oils, not yet anyway. He studied in the country he was born in, then moved here to study further. He used oils from a young age and has never used acrylics. He doesn't like watercolours, which I just don't understand. The lights aren't normally on, that's why I haven't noticed them before. He finds this funny. I tell him that for one of my uni modules I used to sit on the same side of the classroom every week. I thought it was so strange that there was no clock in there. One week I was late and had to sit on the other side of the room. The clock was above the seat I normally sat in. He lets out a short, loud laugh. Oh come on, you're better than that. This really makes me smile, and I try not to shake my head. I'm actually not. I blame this job. I spend so much time thinking, I'm not very aware of my surroundings.

They are of the same palette as his still-lifes. The black of shadows or heavy linen; tin grey with light reflecting; beech wood or resting flesh. The three together, on the gallery wall. Zhang Enli painted buckets. I looked into, onto, at. Each bucket is the focus of each painting. It is standing on its base, or one is on its side and might roll away. Unless the lip is keeping it in place. The backgrounds are dark, but applied softly. There is no threat. An empty bucket is still full of air.

)

Kate Zambreno

—

Appendix K: Museum of The History of Human Suffering

The original reason I began this project was to speak about what was absent or abandoned from the final published version of *Book of Mutter*, yet I have only circled around this. There is a cursory list of these errors and omissions in the back of the published book. I was surprised, when people have read the book, that this is often what they have wanted to talk about.

When I go back and look at this list in a PDF of what I think is the final layout, I realise that there are several words misspelled. I'm not sure whether they were caught at some point. When I wrote the materials for the back of the book, I was heavily pregnant and still commuting upstate for several hours each way to teach. Plus there was an Italian man living upstairs who drummed all day long, and I couldn't think well with all of the drumming, certainly not to proofread. I wrote this list off the top of my head. I realise now scanning this list that I've only touched on a few elements in this entire book, this book that was not supposed to be a book that has become a book.

I realise the major thread, or threads, that were taken out of the published version of *Book of Mutter* mostly deal with atrocity and history. The ethics of paying witness, of writing about another's pain. This is what remains to think through, and yet I am resistant. Still I want to ask myself this question, like I am on trial. Why was I so drawn to documenting suffering in this book about my mother? And why did I remove it?

***

I have been watching the beginning of *Hiroshima mon Amour* over and over again on my laptop, taking notes. The two shots at the opening, the dying bodies, covered with ash, dissolving to the two lovers, their smooth, sweaty, naked flesh. The ash turns to sweat like glitter. What is the effect of this texture, of this layering and dissolve? The dialogue that follows also crosses boundaries, the woman's extreme identification with the victims of Hiroshima. I read somewhere that Marguerite Duras based this woman on the phenomenon of white Western women with broken hearts who flocked to the Hiroshima Peace Memorial Museum in the years after the war. The actress, played by Emmanuelle Riva, is an actress there in Hiroshima to shoot a peace film. We learn, later, that her lover was a German soldier shot dead, and she went mad, she was shamed in the middle of the town square, her head shaved, and she was kept in the family cellar until the end of the war. In a dreamy, lover's voice, the man, a Japanese architect played by Eiji Okada, who has lost his entire family to the atomic bomb, says: 'You saw nothing in Hiroshima. Nothing.' The white French woman says: 'I saw everything.' Then we're in her point of view, with exteriors. 'I saw the hospital – I'm sure of it. The hospital in Hiroshima exists. How could I not have seen it?' The re-enactment of sick women in kimonos in bed, a naked back of a man turns, covered in scars. The man's voice: 'You didn't see the hospital in Hiroshima. You saw nothing in Hiroshima.' She: 'Four times at the museum.' Exterior shot of museum. 'I saw people walking around. People walk around, lost in thought, among the photographs. The reconstructions, for lack of anything else.' She repeats: 'The photographs, the photographs. The reconstructions, for lack of anything else. The explanations, for lack of anything else.' She keeps repeating: Four times at the museum at Hiroshima. The exhibits of a museum: the twisted metal. The bouquet of bottle caps. The twisted bicycle. Objects of horror aestheticised like modern sculptures. 'Anonymous masses of hair, that the women of Hiroshima, upon waking in the morning, would find had fallen out.'

'I was hot in Peace Square. 10,000 degrees in Peace Square.' The woman says to the man, who has lost his entire family because of the bomb. I haven't yet watched this part of the film this time, but I know the woman will repeat, 'I. Am. Hiroshima.' Which recalls the line removed from Sylvia Plath's 'Lady Lazarus', that I have heard read in her stern glamorous dictation in a BBC radio recording: 'I may be skin and bones. I may be Japanese.'

I think it was the chapter on *Hiroshima mon Amour* in Cathy Caruth's book on trauma that made me incorporate it into early drafts of

Book of Mutter. Caruth thinking through the relationship between history and the body. 'What do the dying bodies of the past – the dying bodies of Hiroshima – have to do with the living bodies of the present?' I was interested in how personal experiences of trauma could be conflated with collective suffering. I was interested particularly in the ethics of that conflation, in colliding an individual consciousness with experiences of war and atrocity.

Rewatching *Hiroshima mon Amour*, it doesn't feel like a work about witness. It instead privileges the white Western woman's wartime experiences of trauma and madness. Hiroshima feels like a historical setting to enact her own woundedness. The woman, speaking Duras's words, doesn't seem to be feeling true empathy for the victims of atrocity even as she says, I have felt what they have felt, I have experienced this pain. Even as she says, See my smooth flesh – it is scarred on the inside.

***

Bhanu Kapil's *Ban en Banlieue* differently re-enacts a series of memorials to martyrs of violence, of racism and patriarchy, through the layering of identification and how the body can re-enact and perform history. At the end of the work, encounter becomes ventriloquism – not only the instability of whether the narrator is or is not 'Ban', the brown/black girl walking home in a London suburb on the day of the race riots, but also as Kapil traces the narrator 'I' who becomes the story of the widow who commits *sati* (the ritual act of a widow immolating herself on her husband's funeral pyre). Perhaps this is because *Ban en Banlieue* also asks the questions: How can a memorial have the energy of performance? How can writing pay witness in the present, thinking through bodies within history?

In *The Art of Cruelty*, Maggie Nelson, thinking through this distance and immersion in the work of Sylvia Plath and Kara Walker, quotes Adrian Piper delineating these distinctions: 'Vicarious possession (case where we take one's perspective to be our own) vs self-absorption (where we project our own pre-occupations onto another).'

***

I would visit Doris Salcedo's 1996 installation *Atrabiliarios* at the Akron Art Museum, when I lived in that city, and was working on the book. A ritual space become reliquary. Rectangular holes covered by translucent cow bladder vellum sewn to the wall, the stitches like a body sewn back together after an autopsy. Each niche contains one or two shoes. Shoes sometimes the only means to identify bodies found in a mass grave (the pain of seeing these, a punctum). In her essay 'Against Witness', Cathy Park Hong writes about Salcedo's installations, which utilise ritualistic objects, especially garments and furniture, to recall the disappeared in Salcedo's home of Bogotá, Colombia, but also other dead around the world, a constant dislocated grief. She writes that Salcedo's installations act as a 'second witness' and are not appropriative because they do not show bodies. When writing this, Hong is thinking through Sontag's second book of photography, *Regarding the Pain of Others*. Sontag: the erotic appetite of showing pictures of bodies in pain – the passage in which Sontag writes about the famous photograph of Fou-Tchou-Li, as he suffers from *lingchi*, or death by a thousand cuts. Sontag lingers on this photograph, on Georges Bataille writing of meditating on the ecstasy of this image, the slowness of this extreme suffering. She attempts to understand the contemplation of this image. Not the man, not his pain, but the image, and Bataille's understanding of it.

)

How wary Sontag is of photographs of war. In her tract she writes of how these iconic images of war can fix memory, can actually work against thinking. She critically references Sebald's use of a photograph of the mass grave in Bergen-Belsen in *Rings of Saturn*. A photo originally without context, like Francis Bacon's photocollage of atrocities that he paints from that Maggie Nelson takes issue with in *The Art of Cruelty*. The Bergen-Belsen image in the Sebald obscenely echoing the photographs of other bodily forms in the book (like the masses of silkworms). For photographs of deformed bodies can be beautiful too, Sontag writes. Is that their danger, their aesthetic resonance?

During the early years when I was working on the manuscript, I was reading Elaine Scarry's *The Body in Pain*, an intellectual leftover from my graduate work thinking about performance art and pain (Marina Abramović's *Rhythm 0*, Ana Mendieta's *Rape Piece*, the suspension hangings of Stelarc). I was struck by not only her thinking on the failure of torture methods to provide true confessions, as well as what she writes of the impossibility of empathy, of truly grasping the interiority of a body in pain. How when the body is in pain, subjectivity leaves. One becomes object: 'the body'.

I forgot that when first writing the book, over many years, I was conflating my mother and the Iraq war. Personal and collective history dissolved. How her wake was held during the bombing of Baghdad. Is this why I was so obsessed with the photographs of Abu Ghraib, with why Lynndie England took those photographs? With Alberto Gonzalez's lying, his willed forgetting (the repeated erasure: 'I do not recall.')? With the memos of the Bush administration. With the testimony of The Tipton Three and The Quahtani Logs in The Torture Archive. With the shattering of language in torture, with the dismissal or erasure of the suffering body in official records. Jenny Holzer's Redaction Paintings series, that I saw at the Museum of Contemporary Art in Chicago. How redaction is the opposite of witness. How I wanted to write of how others suffer, how others are erased, how others are forgotten. But my mother too. My mother perhaps most of all. I cut out all of these notes and now I have these other notes. These fragments. And still I will have to go over all of this again, in more depth, at some other time.

KZ, 21 April 2018

CONTRIBUTOR BIOGRAPHIES

Galia Admoni is the author of *Immediately after and then later* (Black Cat Press, 2024) and co-author of *I get lost everywhere, you know this now* (Salo Press, 2024). She has poems in *The Rialto*, *Bad Lilies*, *The North* and others. She was commended in 2023 Primers and placed third in Briefly Write poetry prize 2022.

Louis Bailey is a sociologist by training whose academic work explores experiences of trauma, marginalisation and resistance. He is currently working on his first book, *The Night Run*, which was shortlisted for the Nan Shepherd Prize for nature writing. Louis' poetry has appeared in several anthologies by Beautiful Dragons Press, and his poem-film cycle, *We Rare Things*, was performed at Salford TGDOR 2020. His cross-genre work has been published by SkearZines and his visual work – exploring folklore, invisibility and moral panics – has featured in a range of exhibitions including 'Out in the Shires' (Worcester) and 'Continuum' (People's History Museum, Manchester). Louis is one of eight participants on the inaugural Prototype Development Programme.

Eloise Bennett is an art historian and curator focused on experimental writing, performance, early cybernetic practices and networked listening. She holds a PhD from Tate and Edinburgh College of Art (funded by the AHRC), and has worked with Yorkshire Sculpture Park and Tate St Ives. Her research has recently been supported by the Paul Mellon Centre and Jerwood Arts, and her work has been presented on Montez Press Radio and in *Motor Dance Journal*. She is Curator at Jupiter Artland, Scotland. Eloise is one of eight participants on the inaugural Prototype Development Programme.

Jen Carter (J E Neary) is an artist and facilitator who writes poetry and narrative non fiction, primarily around parenthood, grief and longing for home. In 2022 she won the Metro Prize by the Poetry Book Society, and was awarded the Terry Kelly Poetry Prize. She lives in Newcastle upon Tyne.

Imogen Cassels is the author of *Chesapeake*, *VOSS*, *Arcades* and *Mother; beautiful things*. Her debut collection is forthcoming from Prototype in 2025.

Kat Chimonides is a writer and artist from Norwich. Her practice explores life drawing, the life model in literature, and the nude in visual art. With seven years' experience as an artist's model, Kat approaches her research through the model's gaze.

Katy Derbyshire, originally from London, has lived in Berlin for over 20 years. Derbyshire translates contemporary German writers, including Inka Parei, Heike Geissler, Olga Grjasnowa, Annett Gröschner and Christa Wolf. Her translation of Clemens Meyer's *Bricks and Mortar* was the winner of the 2018 Straelener Übersetzerpreis (Straelen Prize for Translation), longlisted for the Man Booker International Prize 2017, and shortlisted for the 2019 Best Translated Book Awards. She occasionally teaches translation and co-hosts a monthly translation lab and the bi-monthly Dead Ladies Show. She helped to establish the Warwick Prize for Women in Translation, awarded annually since 2017. Derbyshire's translation of Zsuzsanna Gahse's *Bergisch teils farblos* is forthcoming from Prototype.

Helena Fornells Nadal is a Catalan poet based in Edinburgh. Her poems have appeared in publications including *harana poetry*, *The Interpreter's House*, *DATABLEED*, *Gutter*, *Magma* and *New Writing Scotland*. She received a Scottish Book Trust New Writers Award in 2022.

Miruna Fulgeanu is a Romanian-born poet and translator based in London. Her work has appeared in *Poetry London*, *The Yale Review*, *The Rialto*, *PERVERSE* and *PROTOTYPE 2*, among others. She won the 2023 Oxford Poetry Prize and received a Hawthornden Fellowship in 2022. Miruna is one of eight participants on the inaugural Prototype Development Programme.

Zsuzsanna Gahse, born in Budapest in 1946, has lived in Vienna, Kassel, Stuttgart and Lucerne, and is now based in Müllheim (Thurgau, Switzerland). Her literary work moves between prose and poetry, narrative and scenic texts. She has published more than thirty books, most recently *Bergisch teils farblos* (2021) and *Zeilenweise Frauenfeld* (2023), both with Edition Korrespondenzen in Vienna. A number of her stage projects have also been performed. To list only two prizes: she was awarded the Johann Heinrich Voss Prize of the German Academy in Darmstadt for her translations from Hungarian to German in 2010, and the Swiss Grand Prix for Literature in 2019. Katy Derbyshire's translation of *Bergisch teils farblos* is forthcoming from Prototype.

Eiffel Gao was born and raised in Ningbo, China. She completed her BA in English and MA in Creative Writing at Durham University. She's currently based in Shanghai, working as a communications professional. Her poems have appeared in *The Poetry Review*, *The White Review*, *Shearsman* and *Transect Magazine*.

Mica Georgis is a filmmaker and writer based in London. Their films have screened at international festivals including Cork International Film Festival; Outfest LA; LSFF; and Aesthetica. They have exhibited at galleries including the Institut du Monde Arabe, Paris; the Institute of Contemporary Arts, London; and Scroll Galerie, Nantes. Their first film *ISHTAR* is available to watch on BBC iPlayer. They are the founder and curator of *RAT Zine*, a publication of newly-commissioned work by 13 UK-based queer & trans artists, launched at the ICA in London. They are currently on the Conditions Studio Programme, Croydon.

Matthew Halliday is a poet, fiction writer and critic. His first book of poetry, *The Jude Poems*, was published by Seam Editions in 2018, and he was co-editor of the poetry journal *Kaffeeklatsch* with Joey Connolly. He has worked for the campaigning charity The Prison Reform Trust, and is based in South London. *Revelations*, from which this work is extracted, is his first novel.

Jordan Hayward is a poet based in Manchester, who is a founder and curator of Basket, an event series for poetry, art and sound. His poetry has appeared in *The Rialto* and *bath magg*, and he is a member of this year's New Poets Collective at the Southbank Centre. Jordan is one of eight participants on the inaugural Prototype Development Programme.

Hasib Hourani, born in Bahrain in 1996, is a Lebanese-Palestinian writer, editor, arts worker and educator who lives in unceded Wangal Country, Sydney. He is a 2020 recipient of The Wheeler Centre's Next Chapter Scheme, and his 2021 essay 'when we blink' appears in the anthology *Against Disappearance*. His debut collection *rock flight* will be published by Prototype in the UK in autumn 2024, by Giramondo in Australia and by New Directions in the US.

Aria Hughes-Liebling was born in Chicago, IL, in 1994. Her previous work has appeared in *Granta* magazine.

Dominic J. Jaeckle is a publisher, author, and founder of the independent publications project Tenement Press. From 2016 to 2023, Jaeckle ran *Hotel* – 'a temporary home for otherwise homeless ideas' – a magazine for experimental literatures, both in print and online, that hosted works and works-in-progress by some 500 authors and makers. Recent publications include *Seven Rooms* (Tenement Press & Prototype, 2023), an anthology of works from across the *Hotel* series; *36 Exposures*, 'a bastardised roll of film' (Dostoyevsky Wannabe, 2021; Tenement Press/John Cassavetes, 2024); and *Magnolia or Redbud (Flowers for Laura Lee)*, a collection of 'cut-ups' and appropriated verses in dedication to the mother of William S. Burroughs (Tenement Press/John Cassavetes, 2024). Via Tenement Press, Jaeckle has published works by Pier Paolo Pasolini, Mario Benedetti, Dolors Miquel and Reza Baraheni, amongst others.

Rozie Kelly is a prose writer based in West Yorkshire. After reading English Literature and Creative Writing at Warwick University and the University of Manchester, she moved to the little town of Hebden Bridge where she works for the Arvon Foundation, hosting creative writing courses. Her current work-in-progress, *Salt Tooth*, was shortlisted for the PFD Queer Fiction Prize 2023. Rozie is the winner of the 2024 NorthBound Book Award for her manuscript *Kingfisher*. She is one of eight participants on the inaugural Prototype Development Programme.

Alex Mepham is a writer and translator based in York, UK. Alex was awarded the 2023 Northern Debut Award for Poetry by New Writing North, received third place in the 2024 Disabled Poets Prize for Best Single Poem with Spread the Word, and was longlisted in the 2023 National Poetry Competition with The Poetry Society. Alex has had their poems and translations appear in various journals including *Magma*, *The Stinging Fly*, *fourteen poems* and *Under the Radar*, among others. Alex has translations appearing in *Modern Poetry in Translation*, and is a member of the 2023/24 Emerging Translators Mentorship cohort with the National Centre for Writing. Website: amepham.carrd.co.

Lucy Mercer's first collection *Emblem* (Prototype, 2022) was a Poetry Book Society Choice. Her poems and essays have been published in *Art Review, Granta, Poetry Review* and *The White Review*, among others, and she is co-editor, with Livia Franchini, of the publication and podcast *Too Little/ Too Hard: Writers on the Intersections of Work, Time and Value*. She is a Postdoctoral Research Fellow at the University of Exeter.

CONTRIBUTOR BIOGRAPHIES

Duncan Montgomery is a wood engraver from the North-East of England, now based in London. His latest project is an exhibition called 'Parson's Pleasure & the Ponds', which will present his wood engravings alongside archival material on the history of freshwater swimming, curated by cultural historian George Townsend. His poetry has been published in *PN Review*, Carcanet's *New Poetries* series, *The Sunday Times* and *Blackbox Manifold*.

Angélica Pina Lèbre was born in Brazil and has lived in the UK most of her life. Her writing has appeared in *Flash Fiction Magazine*, *The Lonely Crowd* and is forthcoming in *Orange Blossom Review*. She is a Best Small Fictions 2024 nominee. 'What is she to me?' was conceived in the Summer of 2020 during The Columbia Residency Programme. A version of it was exhibited with a companion audio piece narrated by the author.

c.f. prior is an art worker, writer and editor. Guided by a preoccupation with hospitality, mutual dependence and loss, they produce texts, events and objects that undermine attempts to keep us from one another. They are 1/5th of the writing collective We Don't Write Alone. They are a 2024/2025 London Library Emerging Writer.

Oisín Roberts is a writer from Derry, Ireland. Above his desk there is a little printed out photograph that says 'even your favourite label will ultimately limit you – resist the urge', and that is where he writes from.

Rochelle Roberts is a writer and editor based in London. She has written essays, poetry and reviews for various publications including *Studio International*, *PERVERSE*, *Lucy Writers Platform* and *Poetry Birmingham*, as well as in the books *Anne-thology: Poems Re-Presenting Anne Shakespeare* (Broken Sleep Books, 2023), *Glimpses of Community* (Munch Museum, 2023) and *Cusp: Feminist Writings on Bodies, Myth & Magic* (Ache, 2021). Her debut poetry pamphlet, *Your Retreating Shadow*, was published by Broken Sleep Books in 2022. Rochelle is one of eight participants on the inaugural Prototype Development Programme.

James Rodker is a poet and doctoral researcher in Art History. He is 26 and based in Bristol.

Jacqueline Rose is a Sydney-based artist. Her drawings and etchings are in the Collection of the National Gallery of Australia.

Leonie Rushforth was born in Ely in 1956. She lives in east London. *Deltas*, her first full collection of poems, was published by Prototype in 2022 and shortlisted for the Seamus Heaney Poetry Prize for a First Collection.

Irina Sadóvina has done research in comparative literary and cultural studies, and is now focusing on writing and translation. She was born in Yoshkar-Ola, lived in North America and Europe, and now lives in Sheffield. Irina is one of eight participants on the inaugural Prototype Development Programme. Find her work at: irinasadovina.com.

Agnieszka Szczotka is a Polish artist, writer and performer based between London and Grudziądz. She received her postgraduate degree from the Royal Academy Schools, London, in 2021.

Maya Uppal is a poet and workshop facilitator, based in Glasgow. Their current research is a form of creative Art History aimed at exploring objects and archives through different temporal lenses. Their poetry can be found in *SPAM*, *MUCK*, *Mellom Press*, *Gutter Magazine*, *David Dale Gallery* and *Brilliant Vibrating Interface*. Maya is one of eight participants on the inaugural Prototype Development Programme.

Stephen Watts' most recent books are *Republic Of Dogs/Republic Of Bird*s (Test Centre, 2016; Prototype, 2020), from which a film, *The Republics*, was made by Huw Wahl in 2019, and *Journeys Across Breath* (Prototype, 2022), which gathers together much of his work from the years 1975 to 2005. The two poems in this issue were written in 2006 between Inverness & London as part of commissioned work on suicide & mental well-being & will appear in *The Language Of It*, forthcoming from Shearsman in early 2025, and a new book with Prototype is also forthcoming.

Jack Young is a writer and participatory artist living in Bristol. He writes hybrid work exploring land justice, queer ecologies and hauntings of landscape and archive. His debut chapbook is *URTH* (Big White Shed, 2022), he co-edited the book *Haunting Ashton Court: A Creative Handbook for Collective History-Making* (Haunting Ashton Court, 2023) and his most recent pamphlet is *in the country garden/the end of england* (SPAM Press, 2023). He also co-hosts the literary podcast Tender Buttons in partnership with Storysmith Bookshop. Recent guests include Max Porter, Bhanu Kapil, Lola Olufemi, Rebecca May Johnson, Octavia Bright, Melissa Febos and Preti Taneja, among many others.

Kate Zambreno is the author of many books, most recently *The Light Room* (published in July by Corsair in the UK). Their seminal work *Heroines* is being published by Corsair in September 2024. Prototype will publish the first UK editions of *Book of Mutter* and its companion text, *Appendix Project* (from which this extract is taken), in spring 2025. Zambreno is also recently the author of a collaborative book of criticism, *Tone*, with Sofia Samatar, as well as *To Write As if Already Dead*, a study of Hervé Guibert (both published by Columbia University Press). Next is a book on zoos and Kafka, *Animal Stories*, as part of Transit's Undelivered Lectures series, forthcoming in autumn 2025. They live in Brooklyn with their partner, John, their two children, and their dog, Genet.

ISBN: 978-1-913513-56-6